James Baldwin Brown

The Home Life, in the Light of its Divine Idea

James Baldwin Brown

The Home Life, in the Light of its Divine Idea

ISBN/EAN: 9783337251321

Printed in Europe, USA, Canada, Australia, Japan

Cover: Foto ©Thomas Meinert / pixelio.de

More available books at **www.hansebooks.com**

TO THE MEMORY

OF THE BELOVED AND HONOURED TEACHER,

A. J. SCOTT, A. M.,

WHOSE WHOLE LIFE

WAS A WITNESS TO THE TRUTH WHICH I HAVE HERE

ENDEAVOURED TO SET FORTH,

AND WHO FELL ASLEEP

WHILE THESE PAGES WERE PASSING THROUGH THE PRESS,

I INSCRIBE THEM,

WITH THAT REVERENT LOVE

WHICH IS ONLY MADE IMMORTAL

BY DEATH.

I SPENT some days last autumn at a large old mansion in the north of England, where a troop of bright young girls are being trained to a wise and noble womanhood. It was while watching their happy and beautiful home life, and thinking what might grow out of their culture in the homes in which they may one day rule, that I formed the plan of instruction for my own congregation during the winter months, the result of which this book contains. At first it was my purpose to publish some of these discourses separately, and in a slighter form; but the subject grew on my hands as I thought it out, to a more formal completeness than I at first intended; and I have gladly yielded to many very pressing requests, from those whose judgment I respect, that I would publish them in this more complete and permanent form.

My aim has been, as my readers will discover, to study the closest relations, and the most sacred duties of life, in the light of Him whose Incarnation reveals the principle of their closeness and sacredness. In this, and in all regions of thought, I desire increasingly to get as near to this Life as possible; being convinced that the root of the true "Eirenicon" in home life, church life, and state life, lies here. If by these pages I can help any to understand even a little more clearly, and to feel even a little more deeply, how sacred these relationships and duties are in the Lord, it will be a source of great thankfulness to me. The renewal of homes must precede all other renewals in wider spheres, for which we pray. May God hasten it in our times!

JAMES BALDWIN BROWN.

10, The Crescent, Clapham Common,
April 17, 1866.

V.

EDUCATION, ... 119
"Bring them up in the nurture and admonition of the Lord."—Eph. vi. 4.

VI.

THE NURTURE OF THE LORD, ... 149
"Bring them up in the nurture and admonition of the Lord."—Eph. vi. 4.

VII.

RECREATION, ... 179
"To everything there is a season, and a time to every purpose under the heaven. A time to laugh . . . . . . and a time to dance."—Eccles. iii. 1–4.

VIII.

GETTING OUT INTO LIFE, ... 214
"And Isaac sent away Jacob."—Gen. xxviii. 5.

IX.

THE FAMILY MINISTRY, ... 246
"When the ear heard me, then it blessed me; and when the eye saw me, it gave witness to me: because I delivered the poor that cried, and the fatherless, and him that had none to help him. The blessing of him that was ready to perish came upon me: and I caused the widow's heart to sing for joy. I put on righteousness, and it clothed me: my judgment was as a robe and a diadem. I was eyes to the blind, and feet was I to the lame. I was a father to the poor: and the cause which I knew not I searched out."—Job xxix. 11–16.

X.

THE GOLDEN AUTUMN, ... 274
"So the Lord blessed the latter end of Job more than his beginning."—Job xlii. 12.

XI.

THE WHOLE FAMILY, ... 301
"The whole family."—Eph. iii. 15.

I.

THEY TWO SHALL BE ONE.

"*So God created man in his own image: in the image of God created he him; male and female created he them.*"
—Gen. i. 27.

THE substance of the world is formed by the combination, in various modes and under various forces, of very simple elements, the essential nature of which escapes our sight. There is a certain rudimental cell in all organic tissues, which, modified and multiplied, builds up the structure in very fearful and wonderful ways. But this cell itself is complex, it has an interior life, and comprehends diverse elements within its unity. These elements can in a measure be discriminated, but the principle of the life remains a mystery still. The keenest observation can detect no difference between the cell which will grow into a pine, for instance, and the cell which will grow into an oak. A great chemist, who died untimely some years ago—a man who, like Goethe, brought a poet's eye to bear on the structure of things—propounded the idea, which may come to be established as truth some day, that the ultimate atoms of all the substances with which we are familiar in the material creation are really minute bodies, as complex and wonderful in their way as the universe itself—being formed by the arrangement, in various modes, of particles of the one simple elemental substance, which God called into existence by His fiat, and out of which He made the worlds.* Perhaps the poet had a vision of this when he spake to us of

> "One God, one law, one element,
> And one far-off divine event,
> To which the whole creation moves."

Be this as it may, the rudimental element of human society is complex: the family is the cell-germ out of which it grows. Human society is a structure which is built up of homes rather than of individuals; that is, of beings in relation, with sacred duties springing out of that relation, which determine the form and the direction of their action upon each other, both in the narrow circle of

* Lectures on the Atomic Theory, &c., by the late Dr. Samuel Brown of Edinburgh.

the home, and in the wider theatre of social and political life.

Perhaps we nowhere get so close an observation of these simple elemental cells out of which nations grow, as in the solemn social covenant into which the band of Pilgrim Fathers entered before they set their foot on the shore of the New World:—"In the name of God. Amen. We, whose names are underwritten, the loyal subjects of our dread sovereign King James, having undertaken, for the glory of God and advancement of the Christian faith, and honour of our king and country, a voyage to plant the first colony in the northern parts of Virginia, do by these presents solemnly and mutually, in the presence of God and of one another, covenant and combine ourselves together into a civil body politic, for our better ordering and preservation, and furtherance of the ends aforesaid; and by virtue hereof to enact, constitute, and frame such just and equal laws, ordinances, acts, constitutions, and offices, from time to time, as shall be thought most convenient for the general good of the colony. Unto which we promise all due submission and obedience."

It would be interesting to trace this exodus of

the Pilgrim Fathers to its origin, and to show that concern for the purity and piety of their homes was the main motive which drove these men forth from their resting-place in Holland, and set them there, a band of homeless exiles, on the shores of the New World. Forty-one men set their hands to that social contract; and the Christian society thus fashioned has grown into the New England States, and has given both force and form to the development of the great republic of America. But those men were not mere monads. They were husbands, fathers, and brothers; and they acted for those whom God had made one with them, or would make one with them. Each carried his associated human spirits with him in his action and undertaking, and each contemplated the establishment of a secure and honourable home life as the essential condition of the growth of a secure and prosperous state. It is just as impossible to get at the naked human unit—a man disassociated from his fellows, having no duties and no claims—as it is to get at the original elemental substance out of which God made the worlds. "*God created man in his own image: in the image of God created he him; male and female created he them.*" Man never was alone; man was never intended to be alone; man never can be alone. The man who aims at this isolation—who disclaims all the duties and responsibilities which arise out of his natural relations, who claims the right to think only of himself, and to care and act only for himself—the apostle strikes off from the great human trunk, with the trenchant axe-stroke: "*He hath denied the faith: he is worse than an infidel.*"

Let us start, then, with this first principle, that the family is the rudimental human institution, the cell from which society is to grow, and of which the Hindoo had some vision, when he said, "Man is nothing until he becomes a triad—man, wife, child." We can then study profitably some of the more prominent conditions of its healthy order and development; for on this—the soundness and vigour of the home life—the welfare of societies mainly depends.

I may note in passing that we Anglo-Saxons have a special interest in the ideas which cluster around home. Far back as we can trace our ancestry—into the depths of the old German forest, or, further still, into the twilight of the morning land—always this home institution meets us, always the home is the rudimental unit of the state.

The freeman dwelling as a husband, the head of a household, on his own clearing, lord paramount in his own home, with a help meet for him—and German homes early nursed a noble type of womanhood—holding his house as his sanctuary, literally sacred to him as a shrine to its God, is the dominant figure in German society. In that wonderful picture of the German nature and institutions which Tacitus painted as a bitter rebuke to the youth of degenerate Rome, this is the central point on which the whole interest turns. Doubtless the lights are touched in with startling brilliancy, and the shadows are softened by many tones. It was a lay sermon to a profligate age, and he used the liberty of preachers; but we cannot question that the picture in its main features was a faithful one, and we may be sure that even then the home was the focus of all the vitality and energy of German society. Perhaps this large capacity for home life was the feature of the Teutonic nature, which made it the chosen theatre of that higher civilization whose germs the Founder of Christianity brought into the world. It is perhaps this reverence for woman and for the sanctity of homes, which characterised their life even in its rudest stages, which justifies the dictum of Hegel, that "the destiny of the German peoples was to be the bearers of the Christian principles." Nor can we pass by the fact without thought, that the land in which—with all her sorrows and all her sins, and God knows that their name is legion—homes are most rich, most beautiful, most blessed, is the chief seat of freedom, industry, commerce, and those higher influences which are slowly permeating, and fertilising the world.

And let not any lonely and homeless one think that this subject is outside his sphere. The home key-note runs through the whole strain of human life. All love and are loved; and there you have the heart of the mystery. Out of this bond of spirits, from which none are free, and which, blessed be God, often clasps the closest those most shut out from poorer and more vulgar joys, flow all the most sacred duties and experiences of life. Life catches its ruddiest hue from the glow of the household fire. And just in the measure in which men and women, however isolated to the eye their lives may seem, learn the secret of fatherly, motherly, brotherly, or sisterly ministry to the men and women and little ones around them, does their life rise into nobleness and beauty, and become harmonic with the life of heaven.

In fuller development of this thought, let us consider—

I. That the first Father and Founder of households is God.

In all human institutions which have their root in the constitution of our nature, we have to consider two things in order to get a complete view of them—the earthly "*patterns of things in the heavens,*" and "*the heavenly things themselves.*" God made the first man after a divine original, and after a divine original, too, He made the first home. Eve, when her tears rained wildly on the blood-flecked brow of Abel, knew but one pang of the pain with which the deadly sin of His first-born had wrung the great Father's heart: "*Hear, O heavens, and give ear, O earth; for the Lord hath spoken: I have nourished and brought up children, and they have rebelled against me.*" And the cities of earth are but the stained and desecrated images of the "*city which hath foundations eternal in the heavens, whose builder and maker is God.*" God has not borrowed these images—"father," "children," "home." It is heaven that lends to earth, not earth to heaven. The things that *are* upon earth, the things which have root in humanity as God made it, and which are not the devil's work, are first *there.* Heaven but reclaims its own when it takes these images, and applies them again to heavenly use.

When we search the secret of the Divine Existence, and attempt to explore the mystery of God, we are fain to cry, with one of old: "*Such knowledge is too wonderful for us: it is higher than heaven, what can we know? it is deeper than hell, what can we do?*" But God comes forth from the darkness and declares Himself; we begin to see Him and to know Him when He reveals Himself as a Father in a home. The inscrutable things of God we leave until we shall "*see face to face,*" and "*know even as also we are known.*" We cling to the human form which shapes itself in the mist of our blindness, and which grows more palpable and manlike as we gaze. He speaks to us plainly and gently as to children; He promises all that the largest reading of the word "Father" can suggest of benediction. He bids us build our homes and bear the burden of them, if we would win the joy; and He shows to us how He has built His home, has taken all the burden of it on His heart and spirit, and looks to be repaid by its concord, fruitfulness, and bliss.

There is no relationship or experience which God has ordained for man of which He has not set the pattern before Himself. There is nothing which He will have man to do or to suffer of which He has not shown the ensample. There is nothing which He asks man to aim at and steadfastly pursue, which He has not made an end also to His own life. The first sentence of God's message reveals to us a love which takes joy in sacrifice: "*God so loved the world, that he gave his only-begotten Son, that whosoever believeth in him should not perish, but have everlasting life.*" Dreary theologians may argue and wrangle about the Ruler; the Lord, who spake not as the Scribes, told us chiefly of the Father—the Father who lays the foundation of His fatherly rule in a sacrifice which the perfect love alone could offer, and which abides as the ensample and inspiration of all perfect love for evermore. In our humble acts of self-denial, for the good of our dear ones and of mankind, it should strengthen, purify, and gladden us to know that we are treading in divine footsteps, and are so far made like unto the Son of God. How little we care to think of it!

We toil, and groan, and suffer, but we forget all that would glorify our work and pain. To understand human homes, we must lift up our hearts to the contemplation of the divine home. The secret of blessed human homes—and there are blessed homes on earth—is to make such love as His love regnant there, and endeavour to live for and bear with each other, as He has lived for and borne with us all.

It is very wonderful how the heavenly experience has ever anticipated the earthly; for sin made God's home dark and sad before the blight fell upon ours. God had built, not a beautiful mansion only, but a home for His children. It is not enough to say that the world glows with beauty, and is charged with treasures of wisdom to him who has the eye to search them out. It is not a great picture, painted with consummate art, which God has set before us in the creation; it is a home which He has filled with the tokens of a loving presence, and lit with a living smile. Through the whole scale of the creation we find our thoughts and emotions repeating themselves. The relations of human life and its experiences have their images everywhere. Love, which is life's mystery, smiles or sighs through the life of every creature. Even the dead rocks have their elective affinities, and like leaps to like with passion as intense as that which burns in the heart of the most imperious of human loves. All the experiences of man in his home, his joys, sorrows, fears, hopes, and the issues that spring from it, find their analogues in the creation; for all things on earth and in heaven have been fashioned to make this universe homelike for the sons.

The world in truth will only unveil its secrets to the man who has a child's eye for its homely beauty. Those grand demonstrations of the skill and the power of God in the creation which delighted our forefathers fall coldly upon our ear. Creation is alive, and it is just the play of the life of creation which these grand demonstrations miss. A dead limb on an anatomist's table may tell you something of its uses, but one glance at the living limb of the athlete in the arena unfolds the whole. Show me a broad landscape with the sunlight gilding its crests and flooding its spaces, while the purple shadows lie calm in the hollows, and you show me more of God in the creation than is disclosed by the analyses of the whole Bridgewater school. They are admirable as anatomy, and anatomy is admirable for its uses, but no dissection unveils to us the great thoughts of God. "*The living, the living shall praise Thee.*" And why? God is life, and the play of life alone can reveal Him. God is love, and the silver cord which binds all living things, with love for its electric fire, alone conducts and displays His energy, in whom all things have their being, from whom they spring, round whom they circle, to whom they tend, and in whom they rest. It is not a mansion then, not a palace; it is distinctly a home which He has built and adorned for us; and He has come Himself to live in it, that every nook may reveal a familiar presence, and that every grand and splendid feature may wear some touch of homely and therefore lovely grace.

The root of the home and of the home life is love. It was love that made God a creator. From the beginning He who "*was with God,*" rejoiced in the habitable parts of the earth, and His delights were with the sons of men. When the first fair beauty of His home had been stained and withered by sin, it was love, springing up from yet deeper fountains, which moved Him to restore it on a larger plan and at a dearer cost— a plan into which none but a fatherly heart can enter, a cost which only *the* fatherly heart could find strength to pay. And that home embosoms our homes in its wide-reaching arms of tenderness. As we make our homes glad by love and wisdom, we are helping to fill with light and joy the great home of God. I don't think that this thought will be any great hindrance to a man in his endeavours to curb the tempers, to tame the sensuality, to kill the selfishness, which make homes so wretched. Perhaps it may be a great help to him to know that in his efforts against evil he is struggling not for himself only but for God.

Love is simply the need that things have of each other—and souls. You will question my inclusion of things within the charmed circle. But human love has its analogue in that yearning of elements toward each other, which lies at the heart of all the movement and circulation of the world. The image of clay is transfigured in man. God has made things for each other, and God has made souls. They press toward each other. Life is a fragment until they have blended. Love and its reciprocations develope the full form of life. A man's life is rich just in the measure in which he loves and is loved. Things made for each other draw toward each other. They seek communion, they seek to blend with each other in concert for a common end, they seek to rest in each other's love and be blessed. And the coöperation of those who love is the most perfect coöperation, they draw out the utmost from each, and love swiftly repairs the wastes. No man counts expenditures for ends that a beloved one cherishes, and the loss which he may suffer is swiftly transmuted into abounding gain. A smile, a loving look, it is all forgotten. A beam from a human eye has made you richer than Crœsus; you have seen that in a human countenance, which you literally would not have bartered for the wealth of worlds.

Talk of the hardness of the age, the deadening influence of its commercial habits on the noblest and most unselfish qualities of men! Love laughs it all to scorn, and renews in each generation the youth and freshness of the world. And love will renew it. The world can never brutalise itself while a thing so spiritual as love reigns in it. And love *does* reign. In one shape or other, with all our grinding and driving, our sharp practices and close bargains, love is the mainspring of the world's movements still. A stern, hard, masterly man of business, who had realised an enormous fortune, and was supposed to dream chiefly of gold, died one day. They had to search his strong chest to discover the directions for the disposition of his affairs—in vain, till they found a secret drawer, the innermost shrine of the sanctuary. Here we shall find the will at last. They forced it open, and lo! a bunch of faded flowers, and a lock of a woman's hair. And love, noble, unselfish love, moves more of the springs of your daily city business than any of you dream. And love is simple—it is one, whatever be its sphere. Husband, brother, child, friend; there are not many loves. It is one, and be the sphere closer or more distant, if it be true, it is of kin with the love of God.

"*Husbands love your wives, even as Christ also loved the Church, and gave himself for it.*" And what other love was his who moaned over his dead prodigal, "*O my son Absalom, my son, my son Absalom! would God I had died for thee, O Absalom, my son, my son!*" And that brave sister—I know such—left an orphan in the flower of her girlhood, with a young brother of noble promise in charge, cutting herself off deliberately from all the pursuits and pleasures which make young life so sweet, and shutting herself up to constant, it may be consuming toil. Her face the while has grown wan, her eyes have grown dim, and her form has become shrunk and withered in its prime through this high ministry. But she is earning enough to send that lad to college, she keeps him there among the best, and never tells him what it costs—he will never know it till they meet on high. She gives herself, her life, to him; and her one reward, the rich repayment of every toil and pain, is to see him pass to the front rank, and lay his hand on the chief prize. "Sisters, love your brothers, even as Christ also loved the Church." Love is one wherever you find it, and herein it is heavenly, its chief joy, its dear delight, is ministry to the beloved.

And this is the foundation of homes. Souls needing each other, drawn to each other, enter into covenant with each other, to share and thereby bear lightly the burdens, pains, and cares of life.

The first wonderful thing that strikes us in the institution of the home, is that the man and the woman who are the head of it are twain, yet one. Two as the hemispheres are two, but one in the great circle of the world. Man, here on earth at any rate, is dual. The manly and the womanly natures compose together the perfect man, and live together the perfect life. As in the world, so in the home, God establishes at once diversities and contrasts within the bounds of a unity. The twain shall be one, shall belong to each other, shall be part of each other, and yet they shall be twain also; shall act and react upon each other, and develope by their contrasts and differences each other's life. So precious does God hold this influence of human spirits upon each other to be, with all the wisdom, experience, patience, self-control, and self-denial, which spring out of it, that He sets in a home a man and a woman in perpetual presence of each other, so that neither shall be without the stimulus to noble and fruitful living which such a presence cannot choose but give. Mutual forbearance, mutual comfort, mutual strength, mutual guidance, mutual trust; common principles, common duties, common burdens, common aims, common hopes, common joys—here are the materials of life's truest, noblest discipline; here the metal of character is welded and moulded into forms of finished strength and beauty, meet for the Master's work and joy in the great assembly and Church of the first-born in heaven.

And the twain, the dual man, the husband and wife, who form the one head of the home, are so constituted as to supplement each other. It is easy to contrast manly strength with womanly softness, gentleness, and grace. But strength and softness never did much by concert; where this is all, where the higher idea of the home relation, which descends from heaven, is wanting, man hardens into the tyrant, woman is crushed into the slave. Strength has to learn gentleness and gentleness strength in Christ, before either the manly or the womanly perfects itself, and the two can fully blend. Man is a being of two worlds. It is a sore struggle to harmonise their relations and claims, and to see that at heart the two worlds are one. It takes two to do it completely; a home ought to hold fully the promise of both worlds.

The business of life has, without doubt, a hardening influence. The selfishness, the meanness, the wickedness, which men have to encounter in their daily round of duties, the pure worldliness which reigns in the sphere where much of their life-task lies, tend terribly to mould round the spirit a thick shell of indifference, through which the whispers of light celestial voices and the touches of light celestial fingers can find no way. Tell me, busy men, is the ear as keen as it once was to the appeals of misery? is the touch as fine to the maimed and bruised ones who press by you in the throng, feeling feebly for the virtue which once went forth from you, and took joy in the effort to heal and to save? Does life grow larger, freer, nobler daily, more full of promise, more rich in hope? Or does the wheel drag round more wearily, and the spirit cleave closer to the dust? Alas, yes! And the sin and the sorrow of it, women, lie mainly at your door.

Why has the Father shut you within the charmed circle into which the toils, the hard necessities, the fierce storm of the battle are forbidden to pass? Your husbands keep them outside the citadel with strong arm and brave heart, but ofttimes sorely weary and sick of the strife. And you within? Shut up with the fairest and most gracious flowers that God has planted, and the angels tend—these little ones whose angels do always behold the face of their Father which is in heaven; with a state to rule which is all within easy touch of your hand; with books, and flowers, and music, and all lovely things; with a heart which God has made intuitive of great truths, and capable of high resolves; with a sense kept fine and sensitive to all that men get hardened to, by the genial influences which play around your life. Women, where is the courage, the patience, the constancy, the faith, the hope, the joy, fed ever from divine springs, which God meant you to store up at home? Where is that honey of the higher life which the weary soldiers may taste and grow strong again, when they come home strained and sad from their toils? At home! At home for a man, ought to mean, shut up a while with truth, purity, dignity, goodness, and charity, zoned with a cestus of beauty, and dressed in a lustre of love.

Ah! it is fine talking, many of you will answer me. Brave words, and easy to speak, for those who have never tried the strain of a woman's life. Tiresome children, careless servants, tattling neighbours, and a thousand petty shocks and frets, which try a woman's temper, and wear her spirits far more than the sterner strokes and strains of the great battle prey upon the men! Yes! but then you have laid down your sceptre, you have descended from your throne, you have forgotten your spells. A gracious woman has no tiresome children, thriftless servants, tattling friends. Look upon her portraiture, painted by a great master's hand:

"*Who can find a virtuous woman? for her price is far above rubies. The heart of her husband doth safely trust in her, so that he shall have no need of spoil. She will do him good and not evil all the days of her life. She seeketh wool, and flax, and worketh willingly with her hands. She is like the merchant's ships; she bringeth her food from afar. She riseth also while it is yet night, and giveth meat to her household, and a portion to her maidens. She considereth a field, and buyeth it: with the fruit of her hands she planteth a vineyard. She girdeth her loins with strength, and strengtheneth her arms. She perceiveth that her merchandise is good: her candle goeth not out by night. She layeth her hands to the spindle, and her hands hold the distaff. She stretcheth out her hand to the poor; yea, she reacheth forth her hand to the needy. She is not afraid of the snow for her household: for all her household are clothed with scarlet. She maketh herself coverings of tapestry; her clothing is silk and purple. Her husband is known in the gates, when he sitteth among the elders of the land. She maketh fine linen, and selleth it; and delivereth girdles unto the merchant. Strength and honour are her clothing; and she shall rejoice in time to come. She openeth her mouth with wisdom; and in her tongue is the law of kindness. She looketh well to the ways of her household, and eateth not the bread of idleness. Her children arise up, and call her blessed; her husband also, and he praiseth her. Many daughters have done virtuously, but thou excellest them all. Favour is deceitful, and beauty is vain; but a woman that feareth the Lord she shall be praised. Give her the fruit of her hands; and let her own works praise her in the gates."* (Prov. xxxi. 10–31.)

Such women have learnt the spell to which the idle rout of frets and cares cringe down, as the waves knew their Master's presence, and smoothed their foamy crests when he arose. I know women whose hearts are an unfailing fountain of courage and inspiration to the hard-pressed man, who but for them must be worsted in life's battle; whose pure loftiness of spirit, caught from contact with the Highest, breathes calm rebuke on the beggarly aims and hopes, which seem so large when we are down upon the level, so poor when we are up upon the height; whose sweet serenity, like a cool hand, purges the heat of anger and passion; whose stores of thought, feeling, and observation, spread forth with happy art, make home a treasury of pure and elevating pleasures; whose sympathy is strength to the weary, and guidance to the perplexed; and who send forth husband or brother each morning with new strength for his conflict, armed, as the lady armed her knight of old, with a shield which he may not stain in any unseemly conflicts, and a sword which he dares only use against the enemies of truth, righteousness, and God.

I know such women, and, blessed be God, I have not far to seek them; but it seems sometimes as if they were becoming fewer. They could not have been rare in Shakespeare's day, in Spenser's day, in Chaucer's day. There were many of them in the company which gathered around the Lord. But where are they now? Women, gather again around the springs whence the holy women of old drew their inspirations. Live much with God, that your prayers may strengthen your husbands to bear them manlike in the battle, and that you may have some bread which is nutritive of manly vigour, when, weary with the struggle, they come home to you to rest. You live in a charmed circle guarded carefully from the shocks which bruise the limbs and organs of the higher life in those who go down to the contentions of the world. Fill that circle with something that men may honour and cherish, the more dearly because they meet it so rarely in the scenes where they ply their tasks. Set fairly before their sight the noblest, purest, most lovely thing that God looks upon in all His worlds—a woman of gracious, serene, liberal, and chastened spirit. Let the fountain of living waters be ever gushing for the refreshing of the weary pilgrims of the household, where God has trained them by sure instinct to look for it—the mother's heart.

I say nothing here of woman's rights. I have not the patience to do it. Battling for idle rights, while she lets such glorious power slip all unused out of her hand! Wonderful is the power of woman to rule the world, to do what she will with it, if she but cares to wield it. But the one spring of her power is the spring of the divine power, and of the power that lies in all nobleness and goodness, the power to love, to serve, to save. Seize it once more, and the world is at your feet.

Thus far I have spoken almost exclusively of the women, for the home is their realm. But what of the men? I think that the best homework which they can do is to help the women, by patience, tenderness, and cheerfulness, to realize their idea. There is a certain monotony in the household cares, of which the men, whose work calls them abroad, should never be unmindful; the joyful break in that monotony should be their entrance into the home, which needs their presence to crown its life. Busy, energetic men are sadly tempted to think of the high-minded women who have a vision of what the home-life might be, as dreamers; and to treat their vivid sense of the spiritual as a graceful, womanly weakness, with which they have no need to concern themselves, their life lying in a quite different sphere. It is this division of the spheres which is so detrimental, so fatal. Communion of interest, belief, pursuit, is the very life-blood of the home. Unless the husband has the grace to honour in his heart the ideal which his wife is aiming at, to watch her endeavour with tender reverence, and lend a brave hand to carry it up to success, the home will lose its sunlight, the children their noblest nurture, and life its most golden fruits.

And say not, I pray you, that this is pure idealism, and that human homes in such a world as this must pitch their music in a far lower and more practicable key. I know such women; I know such homes; and God sees myriads of them; they are the salt of the earth, and its light. Women, *you* must multiply them, if society is to be saved. And if ideals are bootless, and only daunt and dispirit us, why has God set before us, clear within our horizon, such a life as the life of His well-beloved Son? Thank God that you have such ideals above you far up in the height, which are ever drawing you by their sweet magnetic spells out of the slough in which the devil of worldliness and selfishness is seeking to drown you, burying there what dignity, purity, and nobleness are still left us in the world, to lift our life up above the brutes. Honour these lofty forms of things in your heart of hearts, aim at them in your life of lives. Lend dignity thus to every effort to rule passion, to curb self-will, to master the body, to conquer the world, to cheer and gladden the home with the light which God kindles in the heart which can be satisfied supremely only by His love. And then, as the years roll on, and the family widens, and some, not the least beloved, leave it, to prepare a welcome for the tired pilgrims to the eternal mansions where the "whole family" will be gathered at last, see to it that day by day, by patient, constant, God-directed efforts, your surroundings in the house which God has built to shelter you, grow more into the likeness which heaven as well as earth shall recognise as "a home."

II.

THESE LITTLE ONES.

" Take heed that ye despise not one of these little ones."
—MATT. xviii. 10.

EARTH has no monopoly of the experiences of "home." It is a divine image, having its archetype on high, which is reproduced in whatever is purest and brightest in the home life of mankind. There was the divine home before there was the human. The Father knew His child and blessed him; yea, He foreknew all the pain, the anguish, the joy, which would spring from him, before He sent him forth to found *his* home, and learn out of his own home-experience the secret of his relations and duties to his God. We have seen already that the broad fact of the human home is duality with unity. One flesh, yet twain. One human being, yet two human souls, acting on each other, and reacting; disciplining, developing, and educating each other, and yet the one head of a household; the manly and the womanly natures blending in the one mind which is to rule, and the one spirit which is to animate and consecrate the whole. "*Therefore shall a man leave his father and his mother, and shall cleave unto his wife; and they two shall be one flesh.*" Here is unity with duality; and this in every region is the condition of all the higher developments of life. I say that the idea descended from on high. The last, the perfect, human estate shall likewise come down from God out of heaven. "*And I John saw the holy city, new Jerusalem, coming down from God out of heaven, prepared as a bride adorned for her husband. And I heard a great voice out of heaven saying, Behold, the tabernacle of God is with men.*" The first human estate descended from the same height, and took its place by the same right as a heaven-born thing in this lower world. It was not good that man should be alone, for a hundred reasons, but mainly for one—God would not be alone. What is the history of this earth of ours but the history of the desire and effort of God to blend Himself with humanity—God in Christ seeking the world as His bride, and filling His home with the recovered, the twice-born sons. There is that in God which moves Him to seek this fellowship with free beings formed in His likeness. We recognise reverently the Divine Sovereignty, but it is only another name for the action whose springs lie deeply enfolded within His own being. When He passed by the nature of angels and took on Him the seed of Abraham, that sovereign act was a full manifestation of Himself. From the beginning, in the elder eternity, or ever time was, His Word ranged forward in thought and hope to the creation, and His joys were then by foretaste with His sons. In the hour of the transgression He joined Himself to humanity; and He became in Eden, ere He drove forth the man, the Father and the Founder of the first human home. Suffer me again to warn you against treating these images as vague poetic expressions, whose literal truth is not to be pressed too rigidly home. Poetry, if it is worth anything, is the speech of that real world which is behind the shadows; and on divine lips, at any rate, the words may bear their uttermost meaning to our hearts. These are not terms borrowed from relations and affinities with which man is familiar, to help him to conceive of the reality of those which are beyond the range of his sight. I again insist that it is the human relation and affinity which is borrowed. We do not borrow the word "Father," and apply it to the setting forth of something which transcends description and definition in God. Were that the truth of the matter, the Chinese should be our chief teachers about the Divine Fatherhood; but they have never been able to take the step from the idolatry of the human father to the worship of the divine. No; God lends to us, and but takes His own again when He bids us pray, "*Our Father, which art in heaven, Hallowed be thy name.*"

You may call this theology transcendental, or what you will, but it is the simple truth of the matter. There is no relation which man sustains, no duty which he is called to fulfil, no burden which he is made to bear, no joy, no sorrow, which it is given to him to taste, the original image of which is not to be found in God, and in God's relations to the world. We interpret altogether too feebly the sentence, "*God made man in his own image.*" We let our reverence become slavish, and cramp our freedom. God has come forth to unfold to us the principle of all the duties, affinities, relations, and experiences of our race, in His own life. *"Thy maker is thine husband; the Lord of hosts is His name. . . . . The Lord hath called thee as a woman forsaken and grieved in spirit, and a wife of youth, when thou wast refused, saith thy God." "Is Ephraim my dear son? is he a pleasant child? for since I spake against him, I do earnestly remember him still; therefore my bowels are troubled for him: I will surely have mercy upon him, saith the Lord."* This is the key-note of God's most earnest and tender appeals to His people. Husband, father, child, He knows the truth of these human relations *from within.*

In the home man developes into the triad, and all the higher interest of life begins. This also has its original in God. A lonely eternity could not satisfy Him; He can be satisfied only in what is born, not out of His hand of power, but out of His heart of love. To dwell with beings after His likeness, able to respond to His spirit, as man moves responsive to man, able to dwell with Him in His eternal home, and to make it bright with the presence of His sons for ever, this is His idea of life. When the sons were born into His home, the life of God was manifest. The living Being came forth to walk and talk in Eden with His children, while the rosy dawn lay soft and bright on the young beauty of creation, and the music of the morning stars streamed down upon the throbbing air, and fell like a dew of benediction, "*Behold, it is very good.*" But the fulness of God, the fulness of His thought, desire, and life, was yet unrevealed. There was that within the bosom of the divine nature which creation could neither express nor satisfy. All its floods of living splendour, all its jubilant bursts of harmony, had left, if creation could have rested there, something ever unsatisfied in the divine heart. The children must win an experience, and live a life, which would set them where creation could never enter—in the inner sanctuary of His love. The Adam of Eden did not meet that longing—the Adam of heaven had to be born. And the second, the heavenly man, is born, not of the *will* of God, not of His power, but of a love which could bear joyfully such pains of death as no creature knoweth, if it might but reclaim the wanderers, and restore the sons twice-born to the Father's home and heart.

And the idea works itself out in the sphere of the human. He who was made in the image of God has the image also of this. As Adam was born into God's home, these little ones are born into yours. The life and development of the child who was born to Him became the supreme interest with God, and of all in heaven that is in communion with the life of God. A new and richer development of the life of the great universe began from that hour, when the Lord looked upon the man whom He had made in His likeness, and sent him forth to his high career. And thus all the nobler interest of your life as men begins, when God puts one of these little ones into your arms. Its helpless eyes and hands can reach the inner springs of your being. They can compel you, strong man, all helpless as they are, to gird yourself for a toil which is your sweetest rest, if these little ones are fed by it,— if they grow fair and strong, and rain the sunlight of their joyous tones and glances on your home as your rich reward. Many a hard line which the world has traced, and many a stain of the dust and sweat of its battle which your day's cares and toils have left upon your spirit, gets wiped away ere nightfall by a tiny hand. All is made soft and bright again as the little ones gather around your knee by the home fireside. These little ones! Take heed that ye despise them not.

Little children; not angels, even in the bud, and never to be angels. God made the rudiment of something much greater than an angel when He made a child. It is idle to talk about the angelic beauty, purity, and grace of childhood, and to maunder about them as if it were wholly due to their parents' sin if they do not remain angels through life and through eternity. They were born through Adam, as Adam was born, to sin, to suffer, and to be redeemed. The seeds of it all lie enfolded there within that soft nest of flesh, which is altogether the most rare, the most wonderful, the most exquisite, of all the mere handiwork of God. The parent who does not understand that these little ones are born for a sad and stern experience, is likely to do his best to hand them over, bound and helpless, into the destroyer's hand. The motions of sins will be at work in them with the first motions of freedom and buddings of life; and Christ, "*the Light which, coming into the world, lighteth every man,*" every child, alone can stand between them and a future, at the vision of which, but for Christ and His redemption of these little ones, the heart of a parent might well shudder and fall as dead. Do not mistake them, then, for angels, needing but freedom to soar in empyrean regions. They are men and women, whose life here must be a stern and long struggle with sin, and who must learn to suffer and to conquer before they can soar, whom God puts into your arms in the soft bud of their being; and He prays you to use wise fatherly and motherly discipline with them from the first, as He uses it with you. We talk sometimes very foolishly about the perfectness of Adam in Eden. It was but an infirm and partial perfectness. At the first touch of the tempter, it collapsed and crumbled into dust. Of like substance is the perfectness of these little ones,—a perfect image, a fair promise, a bright prophecy, the fulfilling of which lies beyond this sin-haunted wilderness and the river of death.

These little ones! Not angels, then; on the other hand, not children of the devil, but nurslings of Christ. "Take it, and bring it up for Me." I have no call to enter here into curious doctrinal discussions as to the natural estate of young children. Blessed be God, their estate in Christ has become a spiritual estate, and all their destiny has passed under the rule of His redeeming love. We have buried for ever, let us hope, that terrible sentence of a pitiless Calvinism, "There are infants a span long in hell." I have heard the sentence from the lips of divines, and have shuddered as I heard. Devilish it seems to me, for it makes God malignant as a devil. I humbly hope that no threats, no tortures, could make me bow my knee to such a god. I turn from him to the God-man, who gathered the infants round Him, and took them in His arms, and blessed them, and said, "*Suffer the little children to come unto me, and forbid them not ; for of such is the kingdom of heaven.*" Gladder was He, perhaps, at that moment, as the little ones clustered round His knee and pressed to His heart, than through His whole pilgrimage of sorrows. As the pure fresh morning air, in which the rosy flush is glowing, and on which the meadows have flung their dewy sweets, must the balmy breath of these little ones have played on the Saviour's strained and weary heart. Unselfish, unworldly, uncareful, unfearful, unenvious, ungrasping, unconscious, innocent! What a garden of flowers is here, with the morning light playing upon it, and the air alive with song! Take heed that ye despise it not. It is the garden where, in the early light, you may meet the Master: He is abroad in it betimes, and here you may learn His deepest thoughts, and hear His wisest and most lovely words: *"Except ye be converted, and become as little children, ye cannot enter into the kingdom of heaven."*

Little children. The whole force of the words is here. They soon learn the battle-cries of our conflicts, and shape their puppets after the likeness of our follies and sins. But little children are Christ's own nurslings. They love, and trust, and give, after the fashion that reigns in heaven. Love is their sunlight; they ask for nothing but to bask in it. There is no glow for them when that sun in the home is clouded; there are no clouds for them when that sun in the home is unveiled. They have no possessions which they do not increase by sharing. Give a little one the gift it longs for, and straightway it toddles off in its glee to share it with its friend. Their only idea of having is sharing, till you have taught them a darker lesson. The very birds trust not more joyously the bountiful hand of the Father which is over them all. "Never mind," said a little one once to a father who had his full share of the burdens and struggles of life, and who was lamenting to her that he was too poor to gratify some desire which she had expressed—"never mind, papa, you have enough to go on with." Yes, I thought, when I heard it, "*Out of the mouth of babes and sucklings Thou hast ordained strength, and perfected praise.*"

A whole Sermon on the Mount is enfolded there in the bud of their young natures. It seems to us ideal truth. We read these wonderful words of Christ as though they might come to be living words to us in some far-off heavenly state. Look down at your feet: these little ones are living it. They give not their alms before men to be seen of them; and till you have taught them, they use no vain repetitions in their prayers. They are unskilled as yet to pray for their enemies; and they pray with a beautiful trust and tenderness for their friends. The poor, the hungry, open wide at once their fountains of compassion. The last mite goes as frankly as the first, if the Lord has need of it. They nestle closer to the meek, the merciful, the poor in spirit, yea, the persecuted for righteousness' sake, than to priests or princes. A little one would be more at home at the gate with Lazarus, than feasting with Dives at his groaning board. The only patent of precedence you can get them to recognise is the mark of goodness, gentleness, and nobleness, which God's elect ones bear, and which none see so swiftly as a child. They know nothing of the lore of curses and anathemas; coat and cloak may go as they will, so that inner and diviner things are left. They know not to frame hard judgments; they aim not at a double service; they love to build on the firm rock of commandment; the sands of interest, ambition, and worldly honour are too treacherous for their trembling steps; they consider the birds and the lilies with a joy and a wonder which no hard science has robbed of its enchantment; and they take their daily bread as trustfully and thankfully from the same ever-bountiful and merciful hand. Take heed that ye offend not one of these little ones. Take heed. Offend them, and the Master saith, "*it were better that a millstone were hanged about your neck, and you were drowned in the depths of the sea.*"

And God trusts them to us—these little ones—flowers of such grace and beauty as grow not in the plains of heaven. His nurslings they are,—the dearest objects of His care and love. He has nothing in the universe so precious, so rich in promise, as a little child; and this is the gift which He takes, and trustfully places in our hands. There is something quite awful, when we attempt to measure it, in the trust which God has reposed, and still reposes, in a being so hard, so selfish, so faithless as man. These little ones are God's little ones. They are His chief treasures: they are to people heaven or hell. The future of the universe, the fruit of Calvary, the triumph of His kingdom, hang absolutely on *their* future. They are to fill up the number of His first-born, and crowd the general assembly and Church on high; or the devil is to drag them into his accursed dominions, to fill the home with wailing, and Hades with death. The fiends are watching this garden of Christ; the angels are tending it. But the chief keeper and captain of these little ones is man.

And where is the home where these little ones are nurtured up to the idea of "the nurture of the Lord"? There are a myriad human homes where they are nursed on the bread of selfishness and the milk of passion, where the air is laden with blasphemies, obscenities, or with a worse burden, the blight of an utterly worldly and selfish parental heart; where every fair young bud that might fruit in heaven is nipped and blasted, and foul weeds are forced into proud luxuriance, which will fruit in hell; where envy, hatred, malice, and all uncharitableness, form the atmosphere which enfolds the nurslings; where life grows weary and hateful early; where innocent hearts get charged with evil, and noble passions get poisoned with selfishness, and comely shoots get twisted into ugliness, and God's broad seal of beauty is obliterated, and the stamp of the evil one is branded in its room. Yes, there are a myriad such homes where man is doing the devil's work for God's little ones, to one where they are trained to a noble and comely manhood and womanhood, and are sent forth to their battle, since fight they must, as the knight was sent forth of old when his lady had braced on his armour, with a talisman which shielded him from all impurity, and a strength which made him master of every foe. And yet God trusts them—trust, trust, always trust. Verily, "God loveth the world." He gave His Son, He is giving His infants daily into its charge, in tender pity, in pure compassion. He knows that if He were to withhold them, if He were to gather unto Himself in anger, the flowers which we are ever soiling and crushing, the world, bare of its little ones—those rills of healing, purifying waters which are gushing and trickling everywhere about its sin-parched plains—would go down full swiftly to the pit. It is an awful trust, could we truly measure it, this trust of God to His rebel. "Thou hast wronged and wounded me, and behold I give thee these; take heed that thou despise them not." The reason of this trust we are permitted to look into. Some hints of it we will endeavour to set forth.

I. These little ones are sent to us to make us free of the art and mystery of love, that we may learn through the love of man something of the love of God. "LOVE IS OF GOD, FOR GOD IS LOVE." And love is one. All love that is not self-love has God for its fountain, and Christ for its pattern. It is its essential nature to give itself to and for its object. Communion is its passion, sacrifice is its life. A man is rich and blessed precisely in the measure in which he lives in its current. Hell is, where life is stagnant and love is dead. Wretched and unmanlike they, who have never found that which is dearer than life, and for the love of which they will gladly die. Nay, the brutes teach them a nobler lesson, as was written over Gelert's grave. This is the ray of the heavenly glory that once crowned the father of our race, which lingers longest; and it shines oftentimes with softest, fairest lustre in the most wretched, yea, even the most profligate and abandoned hearts. Among the outcasts, the men and women who are stained with every crime and lust, it is the last glow of the pristine glory which lingers, and sometimes it flashes with intense brightness out of the very depths. The Saviour found its purest fire in a poor harlot's heart. Heaven does not give up its reprobates as readily as earth does. It holds to them, as the Lord held to that poor woman who was a sinner, while one pulse can throb to the touch or thrill to the voice of love.

And God has made it the bond of homes. He will make it the bond of kingdoms and of worlds. He lays these little ones in our bosom, that we may learn the lore of love through tender teachers, and be drawn out by mute but sovereign appeals to know all its toils, its pains, and its bliss. The measure in which we know them is the measure of our being; a man's being is just as wide as his love. And what trinity, save One, knows the mystery so deeply? Husband, wife, child, learning daily fresh lessons, to train them for the love of a wider family, and the great Father, God. Perhaps love is purest and freshest in the heart of a parent, most strong to toil, most prompt to sacrifice, most set on another's good. Strong, stern men, whom the world could not bend from their purpose, may be led by the touch of a tiny finger; there are those at home who can turn them by a silken cord whither they will. Thus the home which is near to man as his own flesh and blood, is full charged with the divinest influences. A man must forget his home if he forgets to love. Love is of God, for God is love. See you not how these little ones unseal its purest fountains, and keep them ever flowing, to draw some tinge of living greenness over the driest and barest life?

II. These little ones are sent to us that we may learn through them the lessons of sacrifice, and taste its joys.

The life of a true father is a constant offering of himself for his children. You would not wear yourself out with your daily toils but for these little ones who are fed by them, and who are lifted up by your patient industry to a higher level of culture than in this life you can hope to reach. And there is no pleasure which you taste so sweet as that which you win for your children. To see them bright and glad is the rich repayment of sore toil and pain. God *will* have us live out of ourselves; in other words, He will have us love; for to live self-enfolded is death. Commerce, ministry, interchange of gifts and offices, is the one principle of life. The home, the thing on earth most near to us, is the main organ of its development. There is an altar of sacrifice whose fire is ever burning in every household, and all the richest and purest joys of the household spring out of the offerings which are laid upon its shrine. In a home it is your power to give which makes your riches, your power to gladden, which kindles your joy. Give nothing, get nothing; sow nothing, reap nothing; bear no burden of others, be crushed under your own. Deny thyself, seek not thine own good, but the good of these little ones, and see how they hasten to shower the smiles which are bright as sunbeams on thy life.

" *Ye know the grace of our Lord Jesus Christ, that though He was rich, yet for your sakes He became poor, that ye through His poverty might be rich.*" The bliss of heaven grows out of that great sacrifice. Study it, drink deeply of its spirit, it is the spring of the most perfect bliss of life. For love transforms sacrifice and denial. The freest and healthiest action of the being is that which is most destructive to the selfishness of self. Wonderful, most wonderful, is the power of these little ones to draw forth the noblest energies of the spirit, and to give them such play as the angels might envy in the poorest homes and the saddest hearts.

There is a poor widow there (I am not drawing from fancy) with a troop of little ones round her; the youngest, a sickly fretful infant, needing constant tending, while the ceaseless toil of her hands just finds them bread. Day after day, the long week through, and often far into the night she slaves,—no, no slave works like her; one hand and eye upon her tasks, and one upon her moaning, restless child. Have you ever seen the look of a breaking heart in a care-worn, life-weary mother's face, when the little ones are crying round her for bread, and she dares not for their dear sakes relax the strain, while the trembling hands retain their cunning, and the will can flog the limbs to their tasks? Have you ever heard her moan for rest, the only rest that can help her, when the heart-strings were strung to breaking-strain, and the cry of the little ones grew too bitter to be borne? I have, and I have seen, too, that somehow still the sickly one got tended, and somehow still the work got itself done. I have seen this, and I have been ready to bow down in that poor home and worship as in the vestibule of the heavenly temple; whence clearer eyes behold love's ministry, and a surer hand inscribes the record which will be read out by tender sympathetic voices at that great day, not unnoted of the King of kings.

These little ones. Bear with them, toil for them, suffer for them, live in their life, be glad in their joy. Thus shall you have the blessing with which God has freighted them, to fill your homes with light and love. How many of the most precious pearls of home, like the pearls of the deep sea, grow round wounds, and are the costly burials of pain!

III. These little ones are sent to us surely to hold up the mirror to our evil habits and passions, that we may learn to hate them as God hates them, and may join the energy of our will to His in the effort to master them, and to put them away.

Eve knew what sin meant, and what sin had done in God's home, when Abel lay dead on her bosom. She knew then, too, what God had meant, and what God had suffered by death. It is the very grandest instrument of man's moral culture, this home institution—these little ones, in whom, if we cherish our vices, passions, and sins, they repeat themselves with startling vividness and ghastly ugliness. Can any horror be imagined more dreadful than that which would seize the soul of a drunken father, not utterly brutalised, if he saw his child mimicking his stuttering voice or staggering step, or beginning while yet a child to tread in stern recklessness the same swift pathway to the pit? There is many a parent who will read these words who would be filled with shame and sadness if he were to see, as the eyes above us see, his children reproduce the tempers, vices, and blasphemies with which he is cursing his home.

And they will repeat them. You are as gods to them in their young childhood. God hath made them to yield *to* you the reverence and homage which He claims *from* you. Alas for the hour when they find that their gods are gods of clay, and learn to slight and scorn, and it may be hate, the parent, whom God made as a parent in the image of Himself! It is the most bitter, the most irreparable wrong that you can inflict upon them, to drive them to fear, to shrink from, to hate, what God made them to honour, serve, and love. Well if it does not shatter the whole framework of their moral being, and tempt them to yield to the devil that passionate devotion whose inspiration is despair. God sets your children in your presence continually, as an ever-present and most powerful memento of the fact and the fatal fruit of transgression. You cannot indulge one passion in your home, you cannot give the rein to one lust, you cannot accept the world or self as your ruling inspiration, but it passes forth into your children and begets its likeness, and then rises up a ghastly image, to haunt you at your own hearthfire. Blessings bright as heaven can send you, or torments sharp as the goads of hell, are these little ones. You may choose to make them the brand of your dishonour, or the crown of your glory; the long joy, or the long shame and misery of your eternity.

·These little ones, take heed that ye despise them not!

And what is it to despise or to offend them? More of this when I come to speak of their education. Meanwhile a few earnest words. Do not let them feel that there is no room for them, no food for them, no love for them, in this wide, bright world. It is an awful thing to let a little one, one of God's little ones, grow up to feel that the world is a hard prison-house, and life a long pain; cuffed, kicked, tossed hither and thither, till the young heart that ought to be so glad nestles near to death, with a quiet sense that it is getting near to all that it can dream of as peace. I read this in the papers the other day. Such things, alas! may be read there most days. Let us look at it for a moment, and try to realise something of what this little one endured.

"DESTITUTION AND DEATH.—Last evening, Mr. Richards, deputy-coroner, held an inquest at the Ship and Shears Tavern, Lower Shadwell, touching the death from destitution and exposure of Ann Andrews, aged eleven. Mary Ann Andrews, of 5 Victoria Place, Shadwell, said that she was the wife of a bricklayer, who abandoned her two years ago, and left her with eight children to support. She worked at a dust-yard for 1s. 2d. a day for some time, but fell into such a state of destitution that she was compelled to apply to the parish for assistance. The parish passed her and six children down to Wisbeach. When down there she asked the parish authorities at Wisbeach for assistance, and they agreed to give her 9s. a week to go up to London. On Monday week they gave her 9s. in advance, and she set out to walk up to London, a distance of a hundred miles, with the children, of whom the deceased was the eldest. On the way they once got a night's lodging at a union; on the other nights they slept in lodging-houses. Excepting the 9s., they had nothing except one loaf of bread, which a lady, taking compassion on them as they walked along, gave them. They arrived in London on the Saturday morning. The deceased frequently complained on the road. When they arrived in Shadwell they took a room at 2s. a week. The deceased died on Thursday. Dr. George Sprey said he was called in to the deceased. He found her dead, lying on the floor of a room in which there was no bed or other furniture. The *post-mortem* examination showed the stomach and intestines to be empty. Death resulted from inflammation of the bronchial tubes, and was accelerated by fatigue, exposure, and want of the common necessaries of life. The Coroner having summed up, the jury returned a verdict that the deceased was found dead from bronchitis and the mortal effects of fatigue, exposure, and destitution."

Think how the morning light, which summons you from a luxurious bed to a well spread board, broke over that shivering, starving little one.

Think how all the glad sights and sounds of the bountiful creation jarred to agony on that hungry, death-weary heart. She might have envied, but that her heart was too numb, the birds and the lilies, and groaned over her fatal inheritance of the destinies of a human child. Methinks there may come to be countries of which the Lord of "these little ones" may say, "It were better for them that a millstone were hanged about their necks, and they were drowned in the depths of the sea."

Think tenderly of these myriad little ones whom the morning light wakes up to hunger, filth, and wretchedness; while the evening shadows hunt them into lairs in which you would not care to couch your beasts. Think of them. You cannot mend it all, but you can do something; you can bless and strengthen the hands that are mending it, and which seek and claim the young outcasts of life with long-suffering patience and unwearying gentleness, because they are the lambs of the fold of Christ. Of all the efforts which the Church puts forth—and the Church is coming more and more to be identified with the Christian charity of the times—to heal the sickness and cleanse the leprosy of society, there is none which claims such honour as the endeavour to snatch young children, by education, by industrial training, by vigilant oversight—true episcopal work—from the pits of perdition which our splendid commercial activity has opened in every town and village in our land.

Take heed that ye despise them not. Reverence their purity, their simplicity, their innocence, their unworldliness. Smile not at it from your superior pedestal, but pray that you may grow into its likeness. Be converted, and become as a little child again, like those grand strong men, the apostolic company. Paul, the aged, was fresh and simple as a child, while his arm was strong enough to shake the world. See that you stain not the tissues and foul not the springs of their young lives by the taint of your vices. How many fretful, puny, crippled children bear through life the burden of the sins of their sires! Do not warp their apprehension of righteousness and goodness by admiring tales of brilliant scamps and triumphant cheats. Beware how you interpose the medium of a hard, selfish, and worldly nature between their souls and the voices which God has made them quick to listen to, and which preach from stars and birds and lilies of the field, and friends, and heroes of the past, gentleness, courage, constancy, and love. Let no gusts of passion storm through your home, and lay these innocent flowers stained and broken in the dust; and tempt them not to think, as the world is tempting us all to think, by what you do and delight in, that Christ was dreaming when He said, *"Except ye be converted, and become as little children, ye shall not enter into the kingdom of heaven."*

III.

THE JUST MASTER.

"*Masters, give unto your servants that which is just and equal; knowing that ye also have a Master in heaven.*"
—Col. iv. 1.

Society, under modern influences—of which, perhaps, the most powerful in our time is commerce—tends to form itself into two hostile camps, each fully armed and on guard against the other; as keen and suspicious as were the combatants, at the most critical eras of the patrician and plebeian warfare in republican Rome. There were two camps in the ancient time, there are two camps in the modern; but between these eras lies the feudal age, and we are the heirs of the legacy which it has bequeathed. The feudal age, far from being, as is popularly conceived, a system of organised tyranny, was truly a system of relations and duties. The scheme was very roughly framed, the duties were very ill observed, as Christian duties are in these times; but still, through the whole, the duty of man to man, with the practical obligations which grew out of it, was the paramount idea. This created a unity in feudal society, within whose bounds, no doubt, classes and interests were fiercely at war, the idea of which was purely Christian. The ideas and habits which we inherit from the feudal age, or rather which we derive through it from a higher source, are a protest against this dire division, and a uniting influence which will in time weld even our complex social system into a higher and completer unity than any which has been hitherto realised in our world. For to this everything tends—unity, in higher and yet higher forms, through long and circuitous paths, but with this end, blessed be God, ever in sight.

But, for the present, the prospect seems a dark one. The two camps are thoroughly organised and sharply divided; the "cause of war" is industry and its fruits. Since the great political question was settled in England by the recognition of the principle of the Reform Bill a generation ago, the social question has passed steadily to the front. They must be blind students of these times who cannot see that this question of capital and industry overtops all other questions, and is the great battle-field of this generation. If any are in doubt of its magnitude and pressure, I would earnestly advise them to study Mr. Fawcett's "Economic Position of the British Labourer," in which the question is stated with convincing force and clearness; though there may easily be wide differences of opinion as to the measures by which he believes that the speedier solution of the question may be assured. Has the workman the right to seek ▬ look for some other fruit of his toil than the bare minimum at which, in this sad world, where so many are always at starving point, the employer can manage to get it decently done? This is the great question which the workmen in Western Europe are endeavouring to have settled, though, no doubt, often in blundering and short-sighted ways.

The science of worldly interests, which probably is a fair definition of political economy, precious as its teachings are, would leave us in a dead-lock unless some help were to be brought to us from a higher hand. If man is to rest in that relation to man which worldly interest creates and sustains—and I use the word worldly in no scornful sense; for, while we live on earth, we have no right to speak otherwise than reverently of the world and worldly things, so long as they observe the limits of their sphere—society must remain two hostile camps to the end of time. The employer's interest leads him to endeavour to obtain his labour at the lowest price at which he can induce men to offer it; the labourer's interest leads him to watch keenly for every opportunity of taking his employer at a disadvantage, and wringing out of him in his needs, when he has a contract in hand and at like seasons, the price of which he feels, rightly or wrongly, that he has been unjustly deprived. The two classes are falling continually more completely into the attitude and relation of hostile armies, each having a power so immense and an organisation so thorough, that their contests cannot but issue in grievous harm and loss to both. I constantly hear men of business speaking very gravely of the position of employers with regard to their workmen, and complaining that after the present·fashion things cannot go on long at all. I am quite sure that the workmen share the feeling. There is deep discontent in both camps, and a conviction that the direst extremities of war would be better than the long continuance of this armed peace.

And there are some who look into and read the word of the Lord, who ask themselves sadly, why there should be two camps at all.

It is complained, and justly, that none of the ancient loyal personal relations between masters and workmen any longer subsist. The men are a great army, and are commanded and handled like an army; and as soldiers, from one end of the land to the other, they obey, not their captains of industry, but their self-elected chiefs. The masters can only deal with them in the gross, and by formal stipulations which are entered into by their commanders, and can never get at them as individual men, having thought, will, and love of their own, at all. It is a true complaint, and sad as true. The old bonds have well-nigh disappeared, and the personal element is being eliminated from the relations of the world of industry; as the leaders of a powerful scientific school of thought are endeavouring to eliminate a higher Person from a wider world. It is said that the men have learnt their strength in combination. Probably so; and they are endeavouring to enlarge it by combination with workmen in other lands. But most certainly capital too has learnt its power, its enormous power, of increase. It understands perfectly the grand style in its operations, and it employs labour upon a scale which renders anything like the old personal relation between the master and his work-people impossible, and the idea of it manifestly absurd.

The fact is that business operations are being reduced to the cold certainty and severity of a science. Men are really, and not only nominally, reckoned by hands, and no longer as of old by souls. And if hands are sought without much thought or care of the souls that should go with them, and of which economical science takes little account, then you may expect hard, sharp dealing on both sides; and every advantage will be keenly seized which will make the hands worth so much more to the souls that own them, and to the souls that are hanging on them for shelter and food. It is the vast scale of business, and the rigid calculations by which it is carried on, which has eliminated the personal element from the relations of the classes. And this vast scale makes vast profits. Tens of thousands are 'thought no more of now than hundreds were in bygone generations. There are firms in our great commercial centres which give away annually in promiscuous charity, to cases which they know nothing and care nothing about, but which are introduced by good customers, a sum which would have been reckoned a handsome income from a large business thirty years ago. And these vast profits are no secret. "The hands" will have eyes belonging to them which will look hungrily at your Goshens, and minds, too, which will ponder much upon the question, why is it that capital, got together in a few years, is making thousands out of this business, while for me a halfpenny an hour is a grand advance, for which, too, I had to fight desperately till I was well-nigh starved to death? This is the question which industry is earnestly pondering, and which will have to be settled on some other basis than the present, if the two camps are ever to be one.

Now it is very easy work indeed for us to rail at political economy, and to paint pleasant fancy pictures of an ideal state of industry, in which the comforts and advantages of the workman shall advance precisely in the same ratio as those of his chief; in which wages shall be fixed by kindly sentiment, and all shall be conducted according to the highest moral ideas. But neither sentiment nor the invocation of the past will help us; the path lies onward through stern realities of struggle and suffering, in which the real interest of the classes must be our guide. We have to thank political economy for laying bare the naked facts and laws of the industrial relations and interests of mankind. We are thankful to be made to understand upon what rigid lines of law the industries arrange themselves; and how any tampering with the fundamental laws of the art and mystery of commerce avenges itself speedily, and for the most part with sharpest stroke on those in whose supposed interests the tampering has been tried.

It is most necessary, too, that the money worth of a man's labour should be settled, by trying where the master's interest in keeping it down, and the man's interest in keeping it up, balance each other fairly. Wages cannot be fixed by fancy or by philanthropy. We must know the point at which the opposing interests fix them, the just measure in the economical scale, before higher considerations, which also have to do with the matter, come into play. The conclusions of economical science are as important in this social sphere, as to an artist is the knowledge of the size, shape, and use of the bones and muscles which he has to show to us clothed with flesh.

Let us know what the science delivers to us as its dicta, and then let us be sure that no good can come to us by dealing with them as other than hard substantial facts, which *will* have recognition, or will exact a penalty, if not recognised, which will leave no room for future mistakes. Love is blind until instructed. Cultivated intelligence helps it immensely in its ministry. Political economy is a kind of horn-book, for the instruction of the labourers in the field of a Christian civilisation. The true and complete relations of men, when they are discovered, or rather developed, will comprehend all their rights, interests, and lawful claims. It is well that these should be subjected to the processes of a searching scientific criticism; let us know them thoroughly, and not be afraid to go through much struggle and suffering, in order to their being established; but let us understand clearly that society cannot rest on them; the body must have a living soul, and that can be quickened and nourished only from a divine spring.

The purely economical basis on which the relations of employers and employed are made to rest, is confessed on all hands to be bringing society to a dead lock. The alienation of spirit, and the restless struggle of interests, which are engendered, have become intolerable. One hears confident prophecies, on the one hand, that our labourers will little by little filter out of the land to regions whose wealthy promise beckons them from afar; while, on the other hand, masters prognosticate the speedy lapse of industries by which our commonwealth has long been nobly distinguished, and the transference of our commercial supremacy to foreign powers. One cannot but listen to such prophecies gravely—there is too much basis for them. And yet there is no need to hear them despondingly, for there are strong signs of life about us yet, and where there is life there is hope. The nation which in successive generations has given to the world the steam-engine, the steam-boat, the railway, and the electric telegraph, is, may we not fairly hope, still far from the beginning of its industrial decline? But the gravity of the present state of affairs cannot be exaggerated, and those who are very far from being alarmists tell us that things cannot much longer go on as they are.

The reason of this is simply, that human affairs cannot long get on without humanity, and that no machine works so badly as the human if treated simply as a machine. I am not so foolish as to enter on the thorny question of the readjustment of the relations of capital and labour, in the introduction to a brief discourse, nor should I in any case feel competent to the task. But one can hardly enter upon the consideration of the subject of masters and servants without looking wider afield, and casting a glance at the larger relations which originally wore an almost domestic form, and on which the welfare and progress of society so greatly depend. And without venturing into the domain of which ministers are held to be constitutionally ignorant, I may be allowed to express an earnest conviction, that if ever the camps of industry are to become one camp again, the old personal relation of loyalty between captains and soldiers must in some way or other be restored. And the thing can be done. There are vast mercantile establishments in which the thing is done—not by kindness, we expect too much from kindness—but by wise, provident, and righteous arrangements on the part of masters, involving no small sacrifices, whereby the workmen are made sharers in the prosperity which has been created by their toil.

The only power which can stand up against

the tyranny which the workmen, driven into a hostile attitude, allow their own leaders to exercise over them—the extent of which fills one with amazement, and which *must* be degrading to the manly nature of the classes which submit to it—will be found in the influence of a master who has learnt the true secret of command in the great army of industry, and knows the art of governing men. There are "concerns" in this country from which no combination could win or terrify the workmen; when such multiply, and become the rule instead of the exception, the problem of industry in a Christian sense will be solved, and commerce in a Christian sense will be saved. And that I may not appear to you to be talking idly in pressing these views upon you, let me shelter myself under the authority of a great name. Mr. Fawcett, in a book which has just appeared, and to which I have already referred, deals with this solution of the difficulty as a very practical and promising feature of the industrial life of our times.

"I am chiefly induced to anticipate the future of our country with confidence and with hope, because each year supplies some gratifying indication, that our present industrial economy is susceptible of a beneficent change. Twenty years since, coöperation was looked upon as the mischievous dream of democrats, and copartnership was never mentioned without provoking the contemptuous derision of practical men. You are familiar with some of the great achievements of the coöperative movement, and before many years have passed, there is every reason to suppose that in many of our largest commercial establishments a copartnership between capital and labour will have been established. It is impossible to exaggerate the blessings and the material advantages which may result from thus uniting capital and labour, for the antagonism of these interests has been fruitful of the most baneful consequences. Some successful schemes of copartnership have been described in a previous chapter. The Messrs. Crossley of Halifax, who employ between four thousand and five thousand hands, and whose carpet manufactory is perhaps the largest in the world, have established a copartnership between capital and labour. They have converted their business into a joint-stock company; they have retained a certain proportion of the shares themselves, and have preferentially allotted the remainder amongst their workmen. The workmen are to be represented on the board of direction. It is manifest that those who are employed in this establishment are placed in an entirely different position compared with the ordinary labourers. The antagonism of interests between employers and employed is at once destroyed, and thus harmony and sympathy will take the place of hostility and distrust. The dull monotony which must depress human energy if no other prospect is offered except to work through life for daily wages, will rapidly vanish; for a man's career will seem to be bright with hope and promise, if he knows that some self-denial will enable him to save sufficient to make him a partner in the particular business to which his labour is applied. It will, of course, be said that such schemes are impracticable, that trade could not be carried on if masters were subject to the interference which they would have to endure, supposing they permitted their labourers to become, even in a modified sense, their partners. But the practical difficulties of the scheme will soon receive a solution. It need only be said that those who have suggested and are making the experiment are men who are unrivalled for their commercial sagacity and ability; they speak confidently of its success."—FAWCETT, pp. 244–246.

I have heard, too, quite recently, that a very large firm of high standing in the city placed in the hands of each of their employés as a New Year's gift, an envelope, containing a per centage, in proportion to the salary, of the profits of the year. They are likely to be nobly served.

They say that the home-life is the rehearsal of the great world-life. Certainly this relation of master and workman began in old time upon the domestic idea. It has fairly broken loose from it now. But surely the relations of master and servant in the home circle, ought to prepare us for the wise and righteous handling of the larger questions of rule and service which vex and distract our times. To the consideration of them we will now proceed.

I. The relations of master and servant spring inevitably out of the constitution of human society, as it has been ordained by its Lord.

It is not good for man to be alone. It is not good for a class to be alone. The mutual relations of richer and poorer, wiser and more ignorant, stronger and weaker, finer and coarser, higher and lower, lie at the root of all the nobler life and progress of society. Developement only begins where differences are established within the bosom of a unity. God has so constituted and endowed man, that these differences are inevitable. Nay, if men are to rule and to serve, there is divine example for it. They will find the image of it in the life of God. One who was God, "learnt obedience by the things which He suffered." The doctrine of equality has not a shadow of support in any region of the universe. Superior suns rule inferior planets everywhere. The very dust has its master and subject elements. The struggle to adjust their relations has left its record in every fragment of rock, every splinter of crystal which you tread beneath your feet. Your gardens have their kingly and queenly flowers, their masses of vulgar beauty, and their troop of unnoted, undistinguished helots for daily office and common use. You cannot get into a region where a level is suggested as God's idea of perfectness. Suppose you cut down all the poppyheads, all the flowers which flaunt themselves so bravely in the sun, as they did in the first French Revolution. What would be the next sight which would greet you? New masters lifting themselves above the level with more bold assertion than ever, of their right to the front rank in the procession, the front seats in the theatre of life.

The deadliest thing to my mind about the socialist theory of society is, not the impiety which has been so constantly, and I believe on the whole inevitably associated with it (for whatever the plan of the universe may be, the Maker of it has not built it to the socialist scale); nor is it the crude and childish principles by which it seeks to realise its idea; but it is the idea itself—the ghastly thing which it would make of society if it had its way. It is as if this great world were just the herb garden of the palace of the Eternal; where men are set like rows of cabbage plants, and have to stunt their godlike nature into the cabbage type, as swiftly and perfectly as they may. Abolish ranks, orders, classes, in society, and you begin at once to dwarf the human, and in the end you destroy all that makes the interest of life and the grandeur of man.

The world in its states, its homes, and its industries, must have both the kings and the subjects, the masters and the servants, the brain and the hands. The lords and the vassals of labour, the masters and servants in homes, grow out of the very constitution of humanity. Men fit into these relations, and are unfitted out of them. These subordinations are not the fruit of evil, they are not the work of the devil in our world. The fruit of evil, the work of the devil in this region is, that we have got the wrong kings. Here are natural authorities and subordinations, the root of which lies deeply imbedded in the nature of man and the idea of society: while the fraud, the force, the natural obliquity of humanity, make unnatural ones; they set men in high places who have no power of rule in them, and ask men to obey when they can see in obedience no reason, and no right. And this—the wrong men uppermost—lies at the root of a great deal of the wrong and misery of the world.

But do not let us be one-sided. Society does not rest quietly in this work of the devil, and mistake it for a work of the Lord. It struggles against it, it strives to right it; and this effort of society to right itself upon the pivot of a true authority and subordination, is the spring of all its revolutions and reformations, and of all the deepest and most hopeful movements of our times. Fools in places of authority, knaves in places of trust, tyrants in places of command, cowards in places of peril; here are the parents of the failures and the miseries of life. Obedience, service, loyalty, men owe to the office partly, to the order of society in whose arch this is the key-stone. But how hard and sore the perplexity becomes when the office is one of high use and honour, the man only useless and base! Rebellious questions rise then in the hearts of the noblest to torment them. They rise more easily in the hearts of the self-willed and reckless, and then they torment the world. How beautiful, divinely beautiful, society might grow to be, were the Lord's elect its captains; were its rulers righteous and its teachers wise, its judges just, its bishops apostolic, its rich compassionate, its soldiers humane! Were none called to yield obedience but where God showed the right to claim it, were the pulses of the common life but harmonious with the pulses of the heavenly life, did progress move to the music of righteousness and charity, the Lord might look on the world which He had made, and breathe over it once more the benediction, "Behold it is very good."

II. The question of good servants is fundamentally a question of good masters, good subjects, of good kings.

Not wholly, but mainly. If God made the relation, it must be so. If God made men to be rulers and men to be ruled, and if He has implanted in them instincts which move them towards these relations, and will allow them to rest in no other, the responsibility of failure, if the results go wrong, must rest mainly with those who occupy the higher position in the scale. It is as though God said to them by the very constitution of society, "Rule wisely and righteously, and I charge Myself with the obedience and welfare of the ruled." And on the whole, if you want to be well served you must be worth serving. Men will not, they cannot, spend their best service on a craven or a fool. Men want inspiration from their rulers, from their superiors, in every way. They want an intelligence which shall bring order into the confusion of their thoughts, an energy which shall stir their languor, an animation which shall fire their dulness, a purpose which shall gather up and concentrate all their power, a magnet which shall draw them up to a higher level of life. A true ruler or master is to his dependents as music is to an army, where every head is thrown back, every limb is strung, and every eye flashes living fire, when the tones of the inspiring battle-march burst upon the ear. And this is what sin has robbed us of—heaven's music. It has turned us out of our parade-ground, to slink through the miry byways of a beggarly world. It is through rulers, men with the instinct and genius of command, that the strains are to reach us again; and when men hear the true ring in the captain's voice, and catch the gleam of the true fire, the fire of energy and hope in his eye, a thrill of joy passes through them; every power stirs and stands attent, they gather around him in troops with loyal devotion, and feel with a kind of rapture that they belong to a living army, with leaders and comrades, with an enemy, a battle, and a prize. Men are born soldiers; they rise to their full manhood when they take service under a true captain in the holy war of industry against loafing, and truth against lies. Bless God if He has set you under one whom you can look up to with reverence, one in whom your aspiration seems to be realised, whose life burns to an intenser heat, and can therefore kindle and nourish your own. These are our captains, the men and women who have carried all that we dream of feebly, and more feebly aim at, into some fair shape of achievement, and who are therefore magnetic to us, and draw us upward by the image of our idea. Give us men and women whose life is fresher and more vivid than that of the mass around them, whose spirit is purer, whose thought is clearer, whose charity is more large and free, and the world will not be long in finding out its captains, who conduct to it through vital channels the fire and life of God.

And if the mass thus watch for these leaders, and greet them when they appear, if they are ready, nay, if they press to take service under them, the main reason why there are so many lazy, vicious, thankless, thriftless servants must be, because there are so many vain, empty-headed, empty-hearted, selfish, and capricious masters about the world. And here I am very anxious not to be misunderstood. We say that good parents make good children, and that if children turn out badly it must be mainly the parents' fault. But it would be manifestly wrong to fix this into an absolute rule of judgment, and to lay the sin of every prodigal at the parents' door. Still less can the slighter relationship of master and servant give reason for any such judgment, which would make the servant's folly the master's sin. A good master may happen to have most faulty servants, and his best endeavours in individual instances may lamentably fail. And yet it will remain true on the whole that the servant is as the master is, and that if after the course of generations things have got tangled and discordant, it is mainly the superior's fault. The essential principle of good service is loyalty, the sense that the ruler is the right man to rule, and that his service can draw forth and discipline the powers. There may be much good service rendered to a vain and selfish master by one who has learnt the habit of obedience, and is self-respectful enough to maintain it. But true service cannot live upon bare duty. The dry bread of duty needs the wine of loyalty and love to bring out its nourishment. Service gets poor and cold even in the warmest and bravest heart, if there be no glow of loyalty to animate it; while in all but the bravest and most faithful under such conditions it expires. Unless the lamp of obedience be fed by the pure oil of a noble commandment, it burns low, motes gather and oppress it, it runs swiftly to waste, and then poisons the whole air with the fetid breath of its decay. We want noble women to regenerate homes, we want true masters and mistresses to regenerate service. Nothing is of higher worth to an age or country than service which is loyal and energetic. Not *next* to great rulers, but side by side with them, on the same level of dignity to the eye of Heaven, stand the great company of diligent and faithful servants of their fellow-men.

III. "*Masters, give unto your servants that which is just and equal; knowing that ye also have a Master in heaven.*"

There is the description of the Christian master, the man who is to restore the fallen relations of rule and service after the likeness of the idea of God. It had all been terribly jarred and jangled in Paul's days. Bad masters, bad servants; no centre of rule, and therefore no circumference of service. I suppose that there never was in the history of the world such a relaxation, such a dissolution of the bands of society, as in the days in which the apostle wrote. Nero on the throne of the Roman world! The old noblesse, who had at any rate some traditions of liberal rule in their homes and on their estates, were well-nigh extirpated; while new men, flatterers, panderers, adventurers of all sorts, were exalted to the high places in their room. The last ounce of labour was exacted from the slaves, and the last grain of corn from the estate, to feed the lustful luxury of the lord in the metropolis. The world has never touched such a sheer depth of degradation, society has never been so near to utter dissolution, as in the days when Paul held forth a divine pattern of all human relations, and preached to husbands and wives, fathers and children, masters and servants, the example of *the* Husband, *the* Father, *the* Master in heaven. And it saved society. The men who got their eye on the great example, and modelled their lives as husbands, fathers, and masters on the Lord's, who set the Lord always before them, and found strength to do justly and love mercy in Him who is just and merciful to all, began to reknit the bonds of society. They held together what was falling into ruin; they saved the world; they are saving it still. The number of men and women who are ruling in their homes with the fear of God before their eyes, and the love of God within their hearts, is the number of elect ministers whom we have for the saving of our nation, and ultimately of the world.

4*

The true principle of the whole lies here:— "*Knowing that ye yourselves have a Master in heaven.*" Deal with your dependents as you would that the Lord should deal with you. "*Just and equal.*" Alas! it is hard to get any fair meaning attached to the terms. The man who has found out the *lowest* price at which a starving man or a consumptive woman will take his work, considers that he has found the *fair* price. The mistress who has found out how much a poor domestic drudge will do by eighteen hours of constant disorderly toil, considers that she has discovered the fair day's work. I should dwell more on the fact that the servants here spoken of were slaves, and therefore peculiarly cast on the master's equitable and merciful rule, but that so much of our labour is done under conditions hardly removed from slavish, that the distinction would lack difference if it were placed in too prominent a light. The slop-workwoman, the West End milliner's young lady, the journeyman baker, the Dorsetshire labourer, might look longingly at the slave's ease and plenty in many a great household in Rome. It is a dark sad subject, the conditions under which so much of our industrial toil is carried on. The skilled artizan or spinner has a position whose comfort many a highly educated drudge in superior regions might envy; but there are whole classes of our countrymen and countrywomen whose lot shows darkly beside the slave's or even the brute's.

Yes, but this master, this mistress, have themselves a Master in heaven, able to deal with them as they deal with their dependents, and if needed, to make them writhe as they make their slaves. This is a very strong, coarse form in which to put it, but it is the only form in which some tyrants seem able to understand it; and there are very terrible sentences to be found in the word of God as to the doom of those who persist in provoking the stroke of the Divine hand. But after all, is He not a name or a shadow? Who is the Almighty? where is He? Men may laugh—they have laughed in all ages—at a penalty so vague as the vengeance of the Supreme. And then there is no help. Masters, lords, kings, must go on tyrannising until the maddened victims rise on them, and tear their hearts out as they did once in Paris; and then when they are quivering in the grasp of a wild devilish mob, they may have thoughts in that last moment that the vengeance of an unseen God is not a matter so far off as they had supposed. But if a man has some dread of this awful Being, and some conviction that He is able to destroy both body and soul in hell, then there is some hold of him. It was perhaps the main hold of the Mediæval Church. It helps us to understand those awful pictures of the torments of the damned, which preachers, painters, and poets brought out with such terrible distinctness throughout the middle ages; and which Dante has fixed in forms which will live in men's imagination while the world endures. One can comprehend how the dread picture of an Ezzelino or a Nicholas in torment might help poor, oppressed, down-trodden serfs of toil, or children of peace, to hold fast some faith in the government of a righteous God.

But we rise into a higher region when men can be brought to believe that God is able to bless them richly, to make their lives glad and fruitful, in the measure in which they rain blessings on those whom He has placed under their charge. Then you have the highest assurance that the rule will have a sacred sentiment of duty in the heart of it, and will bless doubly, servant and master alike. And it is the only security. History delivers to us no record of a successful and permanent resistance to tyranny, a steady development of righteous government, except under the influence of these Christian ideas. And here, too, is a power, if it can be brought fully to bear, which can make wise, righteous, and merciful rulers out of very quiet, common, and by no means heroic men and women. It is a power which can reach all, and has the same influence, the same message for all, for the most absolute monarch, and for the poorest housekeeper who has but one drudge to rule over in her own home. The beginning of all good rule, of all fair and equal dealing with your dependents, is the sense that you also have a Master in heaven; and that the model of your method with them is the method of God with yourself. Study that method, and imitate it as you may.

God is merciful, but not weakly kind. Nothing so demoralises as mere kindness, the indisposition to compel effort, and to look on pain. Love in the heart, command in the voice, strength in the hand,—these are the endowments of the merciful ruler. Know what ought to be done, and have it done, with stern imperiousness if needs be, but always with the remembrance that the servant is the Lord's servant as well as yours, and that an appeal lies to His bar. Let the mercy of a brother sinner temper ever your demands and judgments, as you pray that God's judgment may be tempered to you. But have the right thing done, as God will have the right thing done by you.

He calleth us not servants, but friends. There is no Christian home where the servant is not the friend as well as the servant,—where something has not drawn forth towards the master his own interest, zeal, and hope. Something, I say; but there is but one thing,—God's method with us, and that is intercourse, sympathy, and love. I believe that your dependents watch far more keenly than you imagine for little marks of confidence and interest, and would be thankful in return to give you their confidence, and cast themselves on your guidance, if they recognised in you a true desire and power to draw forth their trust. There are a thousand ways in the close intercourse of daily life of expressing kindly interest and good will, and of enlisting that in your dependents which no gold can buy, and no gold can destroy. "*I call you not servants, but friends.*" But God suffers no presumption in His friends, no idle leaning on the friendship, no mere sentimental sympathies; service rendered faithfully to the full strain is the bond of the friendship, and the continual strengthening of the noblest energies of the nature is its fruit. God surrounds us with a vigilant, but unobtrusive care; never sleeping, but never fretting; never tampering with freedom, but never too carelessly trusting it; guiding by the eye and the hand, rather than by the goad; winning confidence, rather than inspiring terror; bearing much and long, rather than casting off, and leaving the outcast a prey to ever-vigilant and malignant foes.

"*Like as a father pitieth his children, so the Lord pitieth them that fear Him; for He knoweth our frame, He remembereth that we are dust.*" There is a tender watchfulness lest the workers grow over weary, the anxious ones over sad. He does not intrude His counsels and messages on all our moods; we are left to fight with many of them as we may; but He never suffers us to forget that He is not far from us in our dire extremities; and that when heart and flesh fail, He is present with His aids. And I have known a wise, kind word or deed, in some moment of sickness or weariness which none but a watchful and loving eye would have detected, break down a hard, rebellious nature, and turn a careless, heartless servant into a humble, submissive, devoted friend.

I know that all this may seem very dreamy and Utopian to many of you. Perhaps you have fairly given up trying to be kind and considerate to subordinates: the more kindness you show, the more licence they take, and the more trouble they give you in the end. Perhaps so. Will you try a new method? Begin with yourself. Take yourself in hand. Bring your own vain thoughts and stormy tempers into subjection; work the spirit and the mind of Christ into the texture of your own, and then try once more. Or, in the worst case, remember that Heaven might say the same of you and me, and Heaven goes on helping and blessing us still.

"*Then came Peter to Him, and said, Lord, how oft shall my brother sin against me, and I forgive him? till seven times? Jesus saith unto him, I say not unto thee, Until seven times: but, Until seventy times seven. Therefore is the kingdom of heaven likened unto a certain king, which would take account of his servants. And when he had begun to reckon, one was brought unto him, which owed him ten thousand talents. But forasmuch as he had not to pay, his lord commanded* him to be sold, and his wife, and children, and all that he had, and payment to be made. The servant therefore fell down, and worshipped him, saying, Lord, have patience with me, and I will pay thee all. Then the lord of that servant was moved with compassion, and loosed him, and forgave him the debt. But the same servant went out, and found one of his fellow-servants, which owed him an hundred pence: and he laid hands on him, and took him by the throat, saying, Pay me that thou owest. And his fellow-servant fell down at his feet, and besought him, saying, Have patience with me, and I will pay thee all. And he would not: but went and cast him into prison, till he should pay the debt. So when his fellow-servants saw what was done, they were very sorry, and came and told unto their lord all that was done. Then his lord, after that he had called him, said unto him, O thou wicked servant, I forgave thee all that debt, because thou desiredst me: shouldest not thou also have had compassion on thy fellow-servant, even as I had pity on thee? And his lord was wroth, and delivered him to the tormentors, till he should pay all that was due unto him. So likewise shall my heavenly Father do also unto you, if ye from your hearts forgive not every one his brother their trespasses," (Matt. xviii. 21–35).

I believe this. I dare not give up hope and effort for any man with these words before me. Dare you? You may feel sadly enough that you have reached the limit of your powers; but dare you, with that sentence ringing in your ears, say that you have reached the limit of your pity, your mercy, your desire, could you but see the way, to help and to save? Until seventy times seven! until numbers end; and then the fountain of all love and pity is unexhausted still.

Here is the most effectual stimulus to unselfish, unrewarded thought and care for others that earth or heaven can supply. When Heaven found it, and brought it to bear on man, then began the regeneration of society. Much of the work must be thankless, and mere nature finds thankless toil intolerable. Disappointed you must be, disheartened you must be; you will constantly be tempted to say, "I have done my utmost for the thankless fools,—I have shown them constant and unselfish kindness, and now I have done. They may take their own course, and go to wreck and ruin as quickly as they please." Nay, UNTIL SEVENTY TIMES SEVEN! And "knowing that ye yourselves also have a Master in heaven," who has spent infinitely more on you, and is not weary yet, gather up your strength and courage for another effort. Granted that for their own sakes they have no claim on you, do it for God's sake; His claim on you is never exhausted, for His patience and goodness never tire. We shall never dare to despair of our fellow-servants if we measure the patience and gentleness of God. Christ stands in the person of every poor suppliant, every humble dependent, and says, "This is the child of my pity; deal with him as thou wouldst deal with thy Lord in his room."

Rhapsody, is it? Vague, dreamy notions, which can never bring any practical help to such a world as this! Very well; but remember that the world began to be helped, began to look up and live, just when these notions were brought into it. And try it long enough on any other plan, you will but let loose the wolves of greed and revenge to torment mankind. To me, I confess, the longer I live the more clearly is it apparent, that the only practical, powerful antagonist to the demons of selfishness and tyranny which are tearing the heart out of society, is the exhortation with which the text is charged, borne in upon us, as it is, by the life, the death, and the risen life, of the incarnate Son of God.

IV.

THE FAITHFUL SERVANT.

"*Servants, obey in all things your masters according to the flesh; not with eye-service, as men-pleasers; but in singleness of heart, fearing God: and whatsoever ye do, do it heartily, as to the Lord, and not unto men.*"—Col. iii. 22, 23.

THAT which is mainly wanted in human relations, is a principle which shall lift our obligations and duties to each other, above those perturbations which spring out of our personal infirmities, follies, and sins. Each man needs a rule and a motive independent of that variable element, the goodness or the badness of the brother to whom he owes a duty. In truth, we only rise to a true human dignity when our supreme motive and regulative power has its organ within; and when the question, in every claim which is made on our service, is, not how much has such an one the power to exact of me, but, how much do I owe it to myself, as in the sight of God, to do. It is as needful for masters as for servants. How much do I owe it to God to do for my servants, is the master's question. How much do I owe it to God to do for my master, is the servant's. Till this be fairly recognised and established as the Christian principle of all social relations, the " tearing, biting, and devouring each other," will go on to the end of time. It may be a very Utopian principle. And it is quite possible, too, that it may have been much more easy to see the way to the application of it in the good old times, when the relations of both home and business were much more simple and limited than they can be considered now.

There is a kind of feeling in the minds of those who do not care to look the reality of this Christian obligation very fully in the face, that the two parties are now, in a large measure, independent of each other, and that each must contend for its interests sternly, doing for itself just the best that it can. Self-interest, we are constantly told—though there is a higher view even of self-interest than the term is usually held to cover—must in the business world rule supreme. Very well; be it so. But, then, let us shut up our New Testament, and have done with the belief that it has some guidance for us as to the duties and relations of life. Is it possible that there is a great world of human thought and activity with which the purest principles of the New Testament have little or nothing to do? I find it impossible to believe it. Could one be brought to believe it, one might be under grievous temptation to shut up the Bible, and see what Gotama or Confucius could do for us in its room. I live in the hope, though we shall none of us see it fulfilled here, that Christ and the angels will one day look down upon a world of teeming activity, invention, and production, a world of commerce, in which the law of Christian brotherly life shall reign supreme; when the sentence, "Look not every man on his own things, but also on the things of others," shall have a large and noble reading in the statute-books of commerce and on the exchanges of the world. The Lord's reign surely will not dry up all the industry and commerce of mankind. And far as we may be from it in these struggling days, and hard as it may seem to work toward it, in the terribly complicated and difficult times in which we live, do not let us give up the hope and the vision of it. And if, in working toward it, however feebly, fortunes lose something of their colossal proportions, we shall find ourselves richer in honour and love, and eternal gainers by the exchange.

To me there is something terrible in the vision of the constant strife and jealousy of the classes. If the world is to be always fighting this battle—the victims of which, in the sickly bodies and the stunted souls which poverty is ever sending forth into the world's highways, dot our fields and throng our streets—then we may all come to share the conviction of an accomplished German professor, that the gospel must be given up as a failure, inasmuch as it has utterly broken its promise of peace and good-will to the world. If this state of things contents you, if it appears very natural, and on the whole inevitable, that society should be drawn out into this interminable array, filling the air with its battle-cries and the earth with its slain, then the whole gospel must seem to you a Utopian vision, and Christ the great dreamer of the world. But if you watch the strife sadly, and yearn to see it healed, you will throw daily fresh emphasis into the prayer, that men may seek both the motive and the law of their duties to each other, not in the vain, inconstant creature, but in the constant, eternal God. This is the help which Heaven brings to us in our business and in every sphere: "*Whatsoever ye do, do it heartily, as unto the Lord, and not unto men.*" Somehow—how we cannot tell, but somehow—this help of Heaven will be made effectual, and commerce, too, will be saved.

Our present concern is with the servant's duty; the master's has already passed under review.

I. Understand that to serve well is in its way quite as noble and even as grand a thing as to rule—perhaps nobler. Obedience and patience are the choice virtues in the estimation of Heaven. Obedience was one grand lesson of the Saviour's life. "*I am among you as one that serveth.*" There have been those, and not the weakest and most ignoble of our race, who have made themselves servants—not sentimental servants, but servants in a real, hard sense—that they might be more like Him. During the early and middle ages, when the life of Christ had a sort of magnetic attraction, men were possessed with a perfect frenzy of obedience. They put themselves under superiors, they prayed to be ruled—ay, even with hard and stern command: they sought cagerly the most menial offices and tasks, that they might tread more closely in the footsteps of Him, who came in the form of a servant, "*not that He might be ministered unto, but that He might minister, and give His life a ransom for many.*" *Voluntary humility*, Paul calls it; and men sought it with passionate eagerness. But the relations and obligations which we make for ourselves have no blessing for us compared with those which are made of God. The obedience which was exacted and paid in monasteries, and under the rule of chivalry, had one great vice—it was unnatural. God did not ask it of men, God did not bless it. He has made room enough for obedience in the round of our common lives.

> "The trivial round, the common task,
> Will furnish all we ought to ask;
> Room to deny ourselves, a road
> To bring us daily nearer God."

But it may exalt our sense of the dignity of obedience, to learn that some of the noblest of men have voluntarily and joyfully sought it, and have felt that they were liker Christ and nearer heaven in obeying humbly and from the heart some hard and even unjust commandment, than in giving rein to the pride of power in swaying the movements of subject multitudes from a throne. There is only one noble conquest—self-conquest. Servants have a grand opportunity to win it. "*Greater is he that ruleth his spirit, than he that taketh a city.*" Some of earth's greatest, by this rule, must be among them that serve. And do not rebel at the meanness of your service, if mean it seem. They were slaves to whom Paul wrote these words: men and women, boys and girls, bought and sold like cattle, and kept close to their tasks by curses and blows. You know no tasks so hard, so bitter, as those which the apostle taught them thus to elevate into a noble form of divine service, as comrades of apostles and prophets, and of Gabriel, the servant who stands before the throne. Refuse to think meanly of any office to which the Master calls you; despise your post, and you will soon degrade your work. Magnify your office by diligent, faithful, self-respectful service; you will pass up one day to stand among the kings.

II. Remember that the measure and spirit of your service is not a question between you and your masters, but between you and your God.

God meant that there should be good *rule* and good *service* upon earth; good command and good obedience. Things can only go on happily and prosperously when duties to God on both sides are fulfilled. A good master kindles a spirit of loyal obedience which makes service a delight; none grudge toils and sacrifices for those whom they honour and love. But you are not *dependent* on good masters. The law of your life's duty is not dependent on anything so shifting and uncertain as the actions of a man. That is a poor life, a base-life, which is carried on by " eye-service as men-pleasers; " a life that waits on man, sinks itself to the level of a brute's. Man is a god to the dumb brutes, his satellites.; "*but one is your Master*, mechanics, labourers, servants, drudges, shoeblacks—"*one is your Master, even Christ, and all ye are brethren ;*" brethren in equality of service to your heavenly King. These are not brave words only; they are simple, hard, literal facts. The man who serves for Christ's sake in the world's service, whatsoever his task may be, is the equal before Christ of the world's princes and kings. Not that he will be strong on theories of equality. Christ's true servants are weak in theories, but strong in work; slow to assert rights,

swift to fulfil duties; poor in pretension, rich in power. They read such words as these with reverence, and a tenderness which abases pride:—
"*Now before the feast of the passover, when Jesus knew that His hour was come that He should depart out of this world unto the Father, having loved His own which were in the world, He loved them unto the end. And supper being ended, the devil having now put into the heart of Judas Iscariot, Simon's son, to betray Him; Jesus knowing that the Father had given all things into His hands, and that He was come from God and went to God; He riseth from supper, and laid aside His garments; and took a towel, and girded Himself. After that He poureth water into a basin, and began to wash the disciples' feet, and to wipe them with the towel wherewith He was girded. . . . . So after He had washed their feet, and had taken His garments, and was set down again, He said unto them, Know ye what I have done to you? Ye call me Master and Lord: and ye say well; for so I am. If I then, your Lord and Master, have washed your feet; ye also ought to wash one another's feet. For I have given you an example, that ye should do as I have done to you. Verily, verily, I say unto you, The servant*

is not greater than his lord; neither he that is sent greater than he that sent him. If ye know these things, happy are ye if ye do them."

Such are readier to serve the servants, than to claim equality with the lords of this world. "*Servus servorum Dei*" meant something on the First Gregory's lips. But this waiting on Christ for the law and the life of your service gives a fixed and noble principle to obedience, and inspires it. You may reckon on faithful and entire service from the man or woman whose eye discerns the Master while waiting upon you. Masters may be froward and fretful, unjust and hard, careless of your burdens, thankless for your pains. Never mind. Not with them is your account. Their smile or good word would gladden you, and make your service the sweeter; but you are not serving for it. There is a gladder smile which is always raining its light upon you, a good word which carries a larger benediction in its train.

Christ recognises no plea for poor and heartless service on the ground of the selfishness or incompetence of masters. "*Thou wicked and slothful servant,*" will be the greeting of all who think to justify a slovenly service by such a plea at the last great day. When He fails to gladden you with His smile or strengthen you with His good word; when you pray to Him for strength to do some thankless duty, and find it harder to do it through your prayer; when something very deep within you says, "ill-done," instead of "well-done," after you have wrought faithfully and taken little of this world's good for your pains; then work as dully as you please, there is no being in the universe who has the right to call you to account. But while His eye is on you, and His hand sustains, and His promise stands, "*of the Lord ye shall receive the reward of the inheritance*,"—work; ay, work to the top strain. Let your soul go into it as well as your muscles—indeed your muscles will never go into it thoroughly unless your soul drives them. Lay on to your work with a will, men, for One on high is watching your labours, who knows from within the pressure of a workman's lot, and who will lift that workman whom diligence and fidelity have made worthy of His fellowship, to His right hand on His throne in heaven. Hear Peter's exhortation:—"*Servants, be subject to your masters with all fear; not only to the good and gentle, but also to the froward. For this is thankworthy, if a man for conscience toward God endure grief, suffering wrongfully. For what glory is it, if, when ye be buffeted for your faults, ye take it patiently? but if, when ye do well, and suffer for it, ye take it patiently, this is acceptable with God. For even hereunto were ye called: because Christ also suffered for us, leaving us an example, that ye should follow His steps: who did no sin, neither was guile found in His mouth; who, when He was reviled, reviled not again; when He suffered, He threatened not; but committed Himself to Him that judgeth righteously: who His own self bare our sins in His own body on the tree, that we, being dead to sins, should live unto righteousness: by whose stripes ye were healed. For ye were as sheep going astray; but are now returned unto the Shepherd and Bishop of your souls."* (1 Peter ii. 18–25.)

But it must be recognised in all fairness, that the conditions of modern service are essentially different from the ancient; and the principle, though substantially the same under all forms of service, needs to be wisely and temperately applied. To the servants to whom Peter wrote, the question, "how far am I to obey an unjust command?" was hardly a practical one. Slaves, bound hand and foot, whom their masters could torment into obedience at pleasure, had no refuge, no escape. Whatever the command might be, to try to obey it was their only course of wisdom; and their power to obey it would be grandly reënforced by such an exhortation, above all, by such an example as this. But in the case of servants hired by free contract for wages, the matter is widely different, and none are called to martyr themselves beyond a certain point in fulfilling a hard and thankless duty, if they can obtain other and more congenial employment. But none can shut their eyes to the fact, that this feeling of duty to the Highest will help patience and strengthen endurance, and will lead an earnest and self-respectful servant to hold on to the very utmost before saying, "I have come to the end of my patience, I must seek my fortune elsewhere." The service whose inspiration is a morsel of bread or a man's favour, unless God's goes with it, will jib at the slightest hill of difficulty, and refuse the collar at the first touch that galls. But it is a base service, and can do no other than basely; while the man who feels that the supreme question is, "what does my Master *there* expect, and demand of me?" lifts his service to the level of an apostle's; he will not be drawn from his tasks by slight discomforts, nor make his own commodity the one regulating principle of his life. Servants, make yourselves as independent as your masters, by serving in all your service "*with conscience toward God,*" *your one true Master in heaven.*

III. Make it your earnest endeavour to be worth a "double hired servant" to your master, for this is "profitable both for him and thee."

I know that this may seem unsound doctrine in the eyes of servants and work-people; just as in tracing bad service mainly to bad mastership, I might easily seem to preach unsound doctrine to the class which I then addressed. I have said something of what I thought of the great tribe of masters, who throughout England compel the troops of labourers who till their fields to feed like pigs, and herd like brutes. There is one other thing which is as hateful in the sight of God and man, and as noxious to the highest interest of society; and that is a sight which may be seen any day where work is in hand:—a strong, stout labourer dawdling over his task as a sick man with a spark of spirit in him would be ashamed to dawdle; laying a brick daintily here and another daintily there, and then stopping to look at it, and have a chat with his mate before he lays another. And if the foreman, who has a duty to his employer, ventures to remonstrate, straightway he strikes work, and carries his base, worthless labour to the next market, where they will endure his sluggard ways. This to a thoughtful eye is one of the saddest sights to be seen under the sun.

Not that on the ground on which masters now elect to stand, the balancing-point of pure self-interest on both sides, I can see any principle upon which it can be fairly condemned,—that is, condemned in accordance with the principles of action which are laid down by the other side. I suppose that the squire who pays his labourers eight shillings a week, has a valid plea before the tribunal of political economy, in the fact that he can get any amount of regular labour at that price, and why should he pay more? And if the workman answers the employer's complaint, "My strength is my bread and my children's bread; why should I not husband it to the utmost, and spend as little as possible at such a price?" I do not see my way, on the economical ground, to a thoroughly satisfactory answer. I can see, I think, God's answer, as we may gather it from His Word; but I cannot see the world's, on the level to which it is content to lower itself. On that level, master and workman must just be left to fight it out as they can, and the weakest in the end must give in. Paul might have answered the workman's question, why should I put more strength than I can help into my work? with some stirring words:—"Work, man, because God made you to work; because work will be a blessing to your body, mind, and spirit; and because such work well done fits you for nobler work in time. Lay these bricks with a will, and you will be laying nobler stones one day, even the stones of the eternal palace, which God is building to be the heavenly home of truth, righteousness, and love."

And there is many a workman in every gang who feels this, and has as little sympathy as any of us with the sluggard and knave; who likes work for its own sake, enjoys it most when he puts most will into it, and would gladly lay his bricks at double the rate if he dared. If he dared! And who is to hinder him? *"Verily, a man's foes shall be they of his own household."* It is the man who works next him of whom he is afraid. If he shows the least diligence he will report him, and he will have a black mark put against his name, because he is making it harder for the lazy ones to live. The sons of industry afraid of industry, lest lazy worthless loons should be forced to work or starve! O men! things have come near their end when ye organise idleness, and make it your god. The most blighting of all tyrannies is that which proscribes the industry and energy of man. There is no curse which can be laid upon a man so deadly as that which cripples his work; and that is the curse which you suffer your fellow-workmen to brand on you.

The first step on, is for workmen of independent spirit to resolve that they will break it. I know well that the question is not so simple as appears. The workmen say that they must give up their liberty as the condition of their organisation; and that nothing but their close organisation, and the pressure which by their unity they can bring to bear, gives them a chance of success in the great struggle of their lives. This is not the place to discuss how far this close organisation on one side has led to as close organisation on the other; nor to inquire which, in the shock of the associations, that of the masters and that of the workmen, is likely in the long run to win. But I imagine that there is little doubt that the success of general lock-outs, has led the thoughtful leaders of the working men to think more cautiously of the policy of turn-outs; and has prepared the way for the breaking up of a system which has exercised a very positive and even terrible tyranny, for the sake of a very questionable good.

But after all, in this sphere, as in every other sphere, what we want is men—men of independent thought and power of action, who are able to lift up their heads against the despotism of the mob. And whence is the help of such to come? Many subordinate considerations may bring help to such a man. A man's manly spirit; his sense of his right to do what he will with his own, and notably with his own muscle, nerve, and will; his duty to his household, which is constantly made to suffer bitterly through the tyranny of his class, which he lacks courage to defy;—these may all stir him to long for freedom. But there is one grand conquering motive which will sustain him in this strife against those who are closest to him in his daily life, as it has sustained millions; and that is the supreme sense of the duty which he owes to his one Master who is in heaven. Set Christ before you as the Master who claims your energetic work, who demands of right that, whatever you do, you shall do it heartily, as to the Lord, and not unto men, and it will deliver you from all tyrannies, whether of masters or workmen. You will work then only where you can work heartily; and it is hard to believe that a workman, who only wants to do his work thoroughly, will be left to starve in such a world as this. Still there are things which a man must be ready to starve rather than be guilty of, and amongst them we must reckon dawdling through life.

The man who enters into the mind of the apostle, and works as the Lord's servant, becomes worth "a double hired servant" to his master. There are some things—and wise employers chiefly value these—which cannot be bought for gold. No wages can buy that vigilance, that constant, untiring devotion to the master's interests, which a servant who loves the family, and the family life, and is counted and treated as an integral part of it, will display. You get some no-tion there of the "brother's service," which the Hebrew lawgiver estimated so highly. And every servant and labourer should aim at it; for the true dignity and honour of labour is the respect, the consideration, the love, which loyal and faithful service never fails to win. There is no more beautiful and honourable relation upon earth than that of the old, faithful, incorruptible servant, to the master or the firm, in whose service he has spent the strength of his days. Earth holds no more honourable men and women than these, who have made a master's interest their own through a long life of service, have sounded the depths of the virtue of obedience, and honoured the station in which they were set by the Lord. These are the aristocrats, the elect, of labour; and to be among the elect is a pure object of ambition in any school. Resolve to win a place in the illustrious band. Be worth a double hired servant to your master, by a diligence that never flags, and a trustiness that never falters; it will plant your foot firmly on the rungs of the ladder of divine promotion. The man who can serve thus for the Lord's sake will rule one day in the kingdom of God.

And did masters care to attach their workmen

by the cords of love and the bands of a man, we should have more of such about the world. "I have worked many a long year for my master," said a poor workman once; "and I have had child after child born, but he has never once asked after my wife or children." A city missionary of large experience went into a sick workman's room, and saw the master sitting by the sick man's bedside. "You have done *my* heart good, sir, at any rate," said the missionary; "I have been many years in the mission, but I never before saw such a sight as this." These are the bands that knit brother to brother, and make a brother workman, with a soul awake for your service, as well as a hand, worth a double hired servant in your business or your home. Masters, make it your ambition to win this service. Servants, make it your aim to live it. It will be the crown of yóur labour, and will outshine one day all conquerors' crowns.

IV. Endeavour to carry the same independent, self-respectful spirit through all the minor arrangements of your life.

I want you to respect your vocation and its duties too much to let them be dependent on a man's whims, frowns, or smiles. I want you to respect them too much to trifle or dawdle through them; rather make them the means of drawing forth and educating your manliest powers. And when your work is done, and the wage is in your hand, I pray you to honour the fruit of your life's work too much to guzzle it away at the gin-shop, or to squander it on those tawdry bits of finery in which silly women take the same delight that silly men do in drams. Do not let the chief fruit of the toil which God honours as He honours no conqueror's work, run down the sink of a dram-shop. Do not despise it so utterly, do not put it to such shameful shame. One of the saddest things in our social condition—yes, I think, the very saddest—is the fact, that it is constantly proved that skilled labourers, who earn ample wages, are the most reckless drinkers, and keep their families in most miserable ignorance and want. In fact, they earn too much money, more than they care or know how to spend intelligently. Instead of a nice, tidy, cheerful little house, with its bit of garden, its comfortable parlour, and all the means of bringing up a family so as to set them on respectably in life, and put the chance of wealth and influence within their reach, they are content to muddle on in a wretched hovel, which a hodman might grumble at for a lodging. They let the poor wife slave, and the children roll and fight in the gutters, while they swill down their hardly-earned wages at the beer-shop, or every few weeks disappear, Heaven knows where, " on the spree." As a rule, it is not the poorest that are the hardest drinkers; it is the skilled workman, the man who might make his labour the basis of as honourable and beautiful a home life as any that is lived in England—that is in the world.

What large employer of labour, observant of the habits and careful of the well-being of his work-people, is not constantly filled with sadness by observing that his cleverest hands are among the most irregular and unreliable; that these are the men who, like Esau, systematically despise their birthright, selling it, not for a mess of pottage, but for a mess which Esau's hunting dogs would have refused. Such men need no Reform Bill to give them votes; the votes are there ready to their hand. They have but to provide for their households the comforts and conveniences which their earnings will afford, as well, if not better than, those of any other large class of the community, and they will be at once far above the minimum franchise in even a moderate scheme of reform.

Handle your wages, then, as you handle your work, earnestly, with a sense of how much is hanging on it. That lad there, when he takes his place one day among the masters, perhaps among the M.P.'s, will be blessing you for every penny you brought home to spend on his schooling; and you, too, may be watching it and blessing God for it, here or on high. Don't rob him, and don't rob that brave, patient, hard-working wife. Don't be guilty before Heaven of the basest, the most brutal, the most damnable of all robberies—the robbery of a home. This is the worst sacrilege, nay, it is the only true sacrilege; for I don't suppose that the bricks and mortar of our churches, and our holy vestments, go for much in the estimation of Heaven.

And you, servants, respect your work, and your honourable name as servants, too much to be mimicking your masters and mistresses in dress and manner. You are not mistaken for fine ladies, believe me. Nor are you, shopmen, when you indulge in Sunday rings and jewellery, and adopt a would-be fashionable swagger, mistaken for the sons of peers. You lose the one honour, the real honour, which diligence and fidelity win, and which set on the honest brow a broad seal which has never been forged; but you do not win the other. Men and women see through the disguise in a moment, and laugh at it. If would-be fine gentlemen did but hear the pitiless laugh with which their strutting pretension is greeted as they pass by, they would rush home to hide themselves, nay, let us say, rather to find themselves; and to don the modest, simple, cleanly self-respectful attire and air which becomes the apprentice no less than the servant, each according to his class. And these, if the honesty and industry of the aspect mate them, win a silent tribute of respect from all beholders, and are the sure passport to the higher rooms. Obedience, sobriety, industry, honesty, neatness, cleanness, courtesy—these are the servant's graces. And again I say, they are as honourable, as precious, in the eye of Heaven, as needful for the work and glory of God's kingdom, as the most splendid talent, the most masterly genius, which have ever played the chief parts on the theatre of the history of the word. There is no respect of persons with God. The slave with Him is as great or as little as the king.

I have spoken of self-respect. With one word on this I close. The ground of all true self-respect is Christ. If we think within ourselves what fine fellows we are, and what honour and homage we have a right to demand, we may very possibly be left to admire ourselves alone. But, if we humbly remind ourselves of the Lord's thought for us and hope of us, how much He wrought and how much He suffered, because He would not allow that we were fit only for the devil's work and wage, we shall feel stirring within us an earnest desire to become something like what the Saviour hoped—the hope for which and in which He died. That is the fundamental principle of self-respect. We are to respect the Lord's part in us, and hope of us. We are never to feel that it is not worth while to struggle, and never may we dare to think that we are too humble to make it of much account what we think, will, and do. The publicans, the sinners, the beggars, these were the chosen companions of His pilgrimage, and His gentleness made them great. It was the pagan feeling that the gods were too busy with their own pursuits and pleasures, to care much how such tiny motes as men might play in the sunbeams, which lay at the root of the demoralisation of the heathen world, and its frightful despair. Christ does care, He cares quite infinitely,. He cares with a care of which you have no measure but Calvary, how you live, how you win, and how you spend your hardly-earned gains. This is the beginning of the workman's gospel; and it comes out of the straits and the struggles of a workman's home. Christ has joy in your honour as a workman, and sorrows over your folly and shame. Fellow-servant, brother-workman, give Him joy of you; let Him " see of the travail of His soul and be satisfied " in your life. The hour is at hand when He shall lift up the head of the faithful servant and workman with honour, in the midst of the most illustrious company of the universe, in the day of the manifestation of the sons of God.

V.

EDUCATION.

"Bring them up in the nurture and admonition of the Lord."—Eph. vi. 4.

The world is the home which God has prepared for the education of His children. The world that is, is fashioned as it is that it may be the theatre of their education; the world that shall be, the new heaven and the new earth, which will be born one day out of the bondage of corruption, will be the theatre of their developed and perfected life. The whole system of nature seems to have been wondrously wrought to be the instrument of our training; the system of the new creation will be modulated to the key of our perfect and glorious life. But man is everywhere the centre. On him the son, the heir, the works of God in all His worlds attend. Round man, as he stood in Eden, perfect in the natural image of

God, wherein he was formed, the whole creation ranged itself as its natural centre; and in man as he shall "stand up" in heaven, perfect in the spiritual image of Christ, whereinto he is redeemed, the new creation, and all that fills it, shall find the key to their order eternally.

These may seem to be overhigh thoughts of the position and relation of a being so fallen, so shorn of his splendour as man. So thought not He who *"in the beginning was with God, and was God," "who became flesh and dwelt among us;"* and who *"seeing that the children are partakers of flesh and blood, Himself likewise, took part of the same; that through death He might destroy him that had the power of death, that is the devil; and deliver them who through fear of death were all their lifetime subject to bondage. For verily He took not on Him the nature of angels; but He took on Him the seed of Abraham. Wherefore in all things it behoved Him to be made like unto His brethren, that He might be a merciful and faithful high priest in things pertaining to God, to make reconciliation for the sins of the people. For in that He himself hath suffered being tempted, He is able to succour them that are tempted,"* (Heb. ii. 14–18.)

And to him who wrote these words it was no incredible thing, nay, it was the most credible of all things, that the whole creation waited, and would wait, groaning and travailing now, enfranchised and glorified then, on the education and manifestation of the sons of God. God makes all things on earth and in heaven subordinate to the culture and unfolding, through grace, of our divine though sin-perverted powers. Education, the education of immortal human spirits, is with Him the great work of the great universe; for He who made the worlds, and who sustains the worlds, gave *Himself* that He might accomplish it. And this is the work which He asks you human parents to share with Him, and to make your great aim and object, within the little world where you play the god—your home. I believe it to be simply impossible to estimate fully the measure of the Lord's interest in this work, and the cost of effort and pain which He has spent and will spend on it, to be repaid in the day when "*the general assembly and church of the first-born,*" shall be gathered in His home, and He shall see in them "*of the fruit of the travail of His soul, and shall be satisfied.*" I speak of all things as made subordinate to this. In the very hour of the transgression the world fell with man. Man changed his relations to God, and the world changed its relations to man. Because of him, "for his sake," the earth became a wilderness. Fair as it had been in its Eden beauty, the curse fell on it; it grew hard, and stern, and cold; it took at once a form, the reason of which was in man himself. Nor was heaven indifferent. I know not what the cherubim were—indeed, I cannot find that anybody knows. But one thing seems clear, they are the recognised symbols of unseen spiritual powers. They represented to the human eye the unseen might and majesty of the world of spirit, and man's transgression drew them down to blend heaven with earth in the work of human discipline and culture. The tree of life passed under their guard until the long pilgrimage should be ended, and is destined to bloom afresh in the new paradise, which these spirits guard and tend for us beyond the wilderness and the river of death.

In truth earth and heaven join their forces that man's education for eternal life may be a triumph; God's great triumph over the devil, and overthrow of his work. Well may George Herbert in prophetic mood declare—

Education.

    "My God, I heard this day,
That none doth build a stately habitation
    But he that means to dwell therein.
    What house more stately hath there been,
Or can be, than is man? to whose creation
      All things are in decay.

    "For man is every thing,
And more: he is a tree, yet bears no fruit,
    A beast, yet is, or should be, more:
    Reason and speech we onely bring.
Parrots may thank us, if they are not mute,
      They go upon the score.

    "Man is all symmetrie,
Full of proportions, one limbe to another,
    And all to all the world besides:
    Each part may call the farthest, brother:
For head with foot hath private amitie,
      And both with moons and tides.

    "Nothing hath got so farre,
But man hath caught and kept it as his prey.
    His eyes dismount the highest starre:
    He is in little all the sphere.
Herbs gladly cure our flesh, because that they
      Find their acquaintance there.

    "For us the winds do blow;
The earth doth rest, heaven move, and fountains flow.

Nothing we see, but means our good,
    As our delight, or as our treasure;
The whole is, either our cupboard of food,
    Or cabinet of pleasure.

"The starres have us to bed;
Night draws the curtain, which the sun withdraws;
    Musick and light attend our head,
    All things unto our flesh are kinde
In their descent and being: to our minde
    In their ascent and cause.

"More servants wait on man
Than he'll take notice of: in every path
    He treads down that which doth befriend him
    When sicknesse makes him pale and wan.
Oh, mightie love! Man is one world, and hath
    Another to attend him.

"Since then, my God, Thou hast
So brave a palace built; oh, dwell in it,
    That it may dwell with thee at last!
    Till then, afford us so much wit,
That, as the world serves us, we may serve Thee,
    And both Thy servants be."

To this end God has made all creation doctrinal, full of the truth on which He seeks to mould the whole of man's inner undying life. We get terribly perplexed in these days of triumphant science, with the distance to which, so to speak, the living personal Presence in nature is removed. To the child's eye the daily familiar aspects of nature easily connect themselves with a living hand. The language of the Psalms about the phenomena of the universe, describes perfectly the child's impressions, and the impressions of childish hearts everywhere. We have outgrown the childish wisdom; God grant that we may not outgrow likewise childlikeness of spirit and of heart. But simple souls, unversed in the mysteries of knowledge, unpuzzled by the problems which the intellect states but fails to solve, and careless of the prizes which intellect must agonise to win, find the old beliefs still credible. To them it is the Lord's eye which blazes in the lightning, the Lord's terrible voice which in the thunder rolls its warnings over the world. They hear the sound of the Lord's footstep as of old, as the breeze whispers at even among the trees of the garden; and as the morning flushes the dewy air, a benediction seems to fall from on high over the waking world. To them the lilies still wear the glorious dress in which He clothed them; and nightly they watch the unseen Shepherd lead forth on the wolds of heaven His flock of stars. The earth seems thronged, as when the veil was lifted for Jacob, with celestial visitants; still they hear the "sound of the going" of angelic pinions in the mulberry tops; and in the silent mountain solitudes there is the murmur of a life of which this earth is not the only parent—and there the veil seems but a thin one, which hides the unseen workman from mortal sight.

But science rends the veil in sunder, and the living presence seems to vanish. The child's belief faints before the vision of the awful force and magnitude of the powers, which maintain the play of life in the creation, the ebb and the flow of its tidal seas. There is such calm certainty and constancy, there is such orderly inevitable sequence in those phenomena of creation, which seemed to us so fraught with living intelligence, that the thought of a living will fades into the conception of a fixed, formal, unalterable law. Things seemingly the most eccentric, when traced back to their springs, fall calmly into this order, which has suffered no breach since the beginning of creation; an order so close, so absolute, that could a hair or a grain of dust move out on an independent mission for one moment, the keystone of the arch would be shattered, and

"Cosmos" would settle into Chaos once more. We feel ourselves pigmies in the presence of such masses and forces as science unveils to us. It is hard for us even to hold fast the consciousness of an independent will, an independent originating power, when all things around us, to the remotest bounds of the universe, through spaces which thought can but faintly measure, fulfil with such calm, impassive submission the behests of primeval unalterable law.

"Is not man a part of the machine, more deftly fashioned, with more subtle and complicated keys?" is the question which science is ever pressing upon us; a question which some of the keenest intellects busy in this field are not afraid to answer, in terms which seem to us to deny at once the living Man of whom the Scripture speaks to us, and the living God. I feel, and doubtless you feel, the perplexity of the problems which science is daily pressing upon us, and how hard it is to hold fast our faith in the reality of any miracle, of a revealed word, of the power of prayer. And I often turn from the perplexed problem to refresh my mind, and to renew my faith and hope, by the contemplation of the palpable moral meanings and bearings of the great facts of the creation; the visible correspondence between the system of the world, and the workings, the unfoldings, of that inner life with which the Scripture concerns itself, and which grows out of the communion of a living human will with the living personal God.

And I do not mean simply, when I speak of the living presence of a moral Being which reveals itself in creation, that there is a certain parallelism between the fixity of the moral and the natural laws, which makes the method of God's way with us as creatures, the key to the higher method of His way with us as sons. This is a very wonderful aspect of the world. The absoluteness with which God will have us obey the ordinances which His wisdom has fixed for us as creatures, is the sign of the absoluteness which reigns also in the higher region. As well may we eat poison, and expect to be nourished by it in body, as drink, wanton, wrangle, and hate, and expect to grow strong and comely in soul. But I mean further, that there are images of man's spiritual relations and duties everywhere around him in the creation; as though God in shaping all things had looked on to the unfoldings of the higher life—the divine life of redeemed men, which springs out of His personal action on human hearts.

There is not one of the great forms of human duty, there is not one of the great relations of Christian society, which does not find some image and prophecy of itself in the creation. The communion, the mutual ministry, of souls in Christ, the Church the body of the Lord, may each find a fair image of itself in the material organisation of this fleshy body, the principle of which runs through the universe. Things could only have been made as they are with a view to the redemptive work, the accomplishment of which calls forth the highest energy of the Father of spirits, and makes, so to speak, the living God an ever-present actor on the theatre of human history. If we *see* God busy with this higher work, the work of calling, justifying, sanctifying, and glorifying our individual spirits, it becomes easier to discern Him behind all that vast apparatus of force which we name laws of nature; through the whole of which we trace the ideas and purposes, which express themselves fully in the spiritual sphere of our being, wherein we see the Father in Christ, and speak with the living God, face to face, as a man speaketh with his friend. While I see so much in nature which I can only understand when I turn to the Church, and the relations of redeemed souls, for its interpretation, this mass and force, this calm constancy of law, lose their power either to oppress or to bewilder me. The God whom I know in Christ, seems to pass with me into the temple of creation. I have not to stand in the outer court and peer through the veil, to discover what the visible things can reveal to me of the "invisible things of God."

The education, then, of human spirits, the unfolding within them of the divine image, and their purification from the blots and stains of sin, is the supreme work of the universe, the supreme purpose and hope of its King. And God has myriad voices and influences under the control of His hand to subserve that purpose, and to fulfil that hope. The creation is full of His teachings. He embosoms the infant in a world of wonder and beauty, which begins at once, from the moment that his eyes open on the light, to educate, that is to draw forth and enlarge his powers. Everything that meets the eye, the ear, or the touch, is educating them, is leading them forth to a larger apprehension, which God meets ever with fresh supplies. The early education of the human infant is simply the drawing out its power to apprehend, take in, and possess its world. Its first discovery is that hands and feet belong to it. Few things are more wonderful to look upon than a baby beginning in some dim way to consider the question, whether the foot which it grasps with its tiny hand belongs to it, and what this belonging may mean. When at length it has discovered its body, and fairly occupied it, it begins straightway to discover its world. The whole system of things around it is a temptation to discovery. There is an ever-widening horizon; every object that it sees, every tone that it hears, but introduces the eye and the ear to some braver object or richer tone, which lie dimly as yet on the bounds of its horizon, but which it must reach and include within its field. Creation is like a great magnet, continually drawing out the powers. And as they go forth they grow strong, they range boldly round a wider and yet wider circuit, and everything which they discover is a stimulus to new quest, with no limit in sight but God.

Perhaps, though, I have spoken hastily in saying that the child's first discovery is that hands and feet belong to it. The first thing which an infant discovers in the universe is love. God's order of the world is in every possible form a protest against isolation, a witness against the self as the starting-point of life. The first impression on the young child's heart, as the mother's proud and tender glances rest on it, is the sense of belonging. There is one to whom it belongs, there is one who belongs to it, on whose care it reposes, in whose love it nestles, before it has taken in an impression about either body or world. The inner world, after all, is the first world that it meets with; and the mother's love, from the first moment, begins its training for the love of man and the love of God. God is nearer to it in that mother's glance and touch, than in anything which concerns its life as a creature of this world. And, oh, how tender should be the glance, how soft should be the touch, which have to speak for Him! The mother's love is just the tuning of the inward ear, to catch at length and interpret the tones of the great Father's voice. Mothers! touch tenderly this delicate tympanum, which, rudely struck or harshly jarred, may be deaf through life to all the higher voices of man and of God.

These thoughts reveal to us the essential principle of all education, the drawing forth the powers to discern so much of fact and truth as they are fitted to take in. It is the process which the Divine Teacher employs through life on our education. That which a man finds, which he discovers by the use of his powers, guided but not superseded by the teacher's, *that* he possesses, and that alone. He is not a receptacle to be filled with knowledge; he is a living organ to be drawn forth to discover it. Truth meets the seeker, just when his search, his desire, is strong enough to take possession of the prize. The pouring in system, as if young souls were jars in which the honey of knowledge could be easily stored for profitable use, flies in the face of the method of Providence. The drawing forth the faculty is the first half of knowledge, and the end of knowledge when won, is the leading forth the faculties to a fresh discovery of a larger store.

And why, with such a grand apparatus of education at his command, does not God keep the work in His own hand, and under His own exclusive charge? It is the thing which He chiefly cares for, and for which He maintains the world. All things that are, from hyssop on the wall to the stars that cluster on the dim bounds of the universe, are His instruments for the education of His child. But the supreme power seems to be lodged with man. As far as outward beings and things are concerned, there is nothing in the world whose influence in the education of man can compare with the human. Man, after all, is the educator to whom God has committed His child. The work of the creation is vague and partial, the influence of man is intimate and supreme. Man can either choke or clear the channels by which the objects of creation reach and draw forth the powers. Nay—and it is an awful thought—how much may man do to choke or keep open the channels for the approach of God! Man may blind the eye and seal the ear of childhood to all that is holy and beautiful in the universe; man may so vitiate the sense, that the world to its young denizen shall seem like a grim prison, or a loathsome charnel-house, full of clanking chains, or "of dead men's bones and all uncleanness." And yet the Almighty Father sends His young nurselings hither by millions, generation after generation. He puts them under the absolute rule of those who can teach them to hate Him, to blaspheme His name with their infant lips, and mimic with their infant powers the vices and the crimes with which their manhood will defile and devastate His world.

It is a dread mystery—this trust of the most precious thing which God holds to man, to be feebly nursed to a godly maturity by the best of men, to be mightily warped and debased to ungodly foulness and deformity by the worst. And how stand the worst to the best, in proportion, in all ages of the world? And the trust goes on widening ever, and with it, we are tempted to say, widens still the folly, the sin, the misery of mankind. It is but a little way that we can hope to see into the heart of this mystery—why God trusts so freely beings such as we are, with the education of spirits who are to people heaven or hell; and *which* they are to people, seems to depend in fearful measure upon us.

He has parents to educate as well as children; *that* helps us some way to the understanding of the mystery. With many a hard sinner the only hold that God has upon him is his child. The institution of the home was God's great lesson to man on the meaning and fruit of transgression. When the first transgressors had a home to rule, and children to wound and wrong them, they understood, as no teaching could have made them understand, what had happened through them in the home of the Lord. The lineaments of their own evil reproduced themselves in their offspring; and in the discipline which they learnt to exercise, in sheer necessity, they discovered the key to the discipline of God. God would make man His fellow-helper in the work of education; He first made man His fellow-sufferer as a father in the experience of the sins and sorrows of his child.

This reflex action of education on the parent is not the least momentous feature of it. God seeks to educate us by trusting us—by calling us to high duties, by laying on us grave responsibilities. And He chooses deliberately the high results which may flow from this lofty method, with the possibility, nay, the certainty, of the dark mischiefs which sin will take occasion to work by it, rather than content Himself with the more sure, though more moderate and common results which might issue from a method in a lower key.

But there is another aspect of the matter at which for the moment we must glance. It is very wonderful on the part of God that He should put such trust in man. Is there nothing wonderful in the fact that man should accept such trust from God? I mean the man who understands all that it involves, and sees plainly its possible issues. There is something very terrible in the mission of a prophet or an apostle, who knows that his word must be "*a savour of life unto life, or of death unto death*," making salvation doubly blessed, or perdition doubly damned. It is a mission which in a measure the parent shares. "*Who is sufficient for these things*," the training of these young immortals? Who dares to put a hasty hand to such a sacred ark of God as this? Nay, who could rest in the prospect of training children after his own image, to be only as wise, as true, as noble, as pure, as good as himself? Is it that we may reproduce our mental and moral image in our children that God entrusts them to us, that we may help to fill His universe with such fractured and distorted images of our Maker, as, alas! we wear? This opens to us the real question, and sets us on the threshold of the true work of education, the first work, the fundamental work. This, well done, makes all other elements of a complete education wholly subordinate; and this undone, makes the most splendid genius but a baleful prodigy, and the widest knowledge but a dreary and pestilential waste.

I have said that of all that is *without* a child

there is no influence comparable with the human. The parent's power, looking on it from without, seems to be well-nigh absolute, either to nurture and develop, or to corrupt and destroy. The issue seems to be in our hands, and who dares bear the burden? Who dares undertake the main charge of the nurture of children with such a nature within them, with a world of such fearful temptation around them, and with heaven and hell as their bourne in sight? Well may a godly parent tremble at the prospect; as Moses trembled, as Isaiah trembled, as Paul trembled, before the threshold of a mission, which bore in its bosom such issues for man through time and through eternity.

There is something very solemn in the conception of the nature and pressure of this burden, to which Moses gives expression in the following passage. It shows us how much he was willing to bear, if he might but find strength to be a fellow-worker with God. *"Then Moses heard the people weep throughout their families, every man in the door of his tent; and the anger of the Lord was kindled greatly: Moses also was displeased. And Moses said unto the Lord, Wherefore hast Thou afflicted Thy servant? and wherefore have*

I not found favour in Thy sight, that Thou layest the burden of all this people upon me? Have I conceived all this people? have I begotten them, that Thou shouldst say unto me, Carry them in thy bosom, as a nursing father beareth the sucking child, unto the land which Thou swarest unto their fathers? Whence should I have flesh to give unto all this people? for they weep unto me, saying, Give us flesh, that we may eat. I am not able to bear all this people alone, because it is too heavy for me. And if Thou deal thus with me, kill me, I pray Thee, out of hand, if I have found favour in Thy sight; and let me not see my wretchedness" (Numb. xi. 10-15).

But here the question arises, the vital question, is the main charge after all with man? Is the nearest, the most intimate, the most powerful of the influences which from the first are at work upon the child, the influence of the parent? Outwardly it is palpably so. But is there no inward influence which can claim the supremacy, no unseen guide and teacher who can take the crushing weight of the burden out of our hands? This is the question of questions in the matter of Christian education, and on the answer to it the very possibility of any education in a high sense depends. Is there a light that, "coming into the world, lighteth every man," every child? Is there a light in that young infant, shining in the first dawnings of consciousness, and striving against the darkness? If you answer me, "There was once such a light in man, but the light was lost in the hour of the transgression, and we can only bring the young child to Christ, if perchance He may rekindle it," then, alas! for you, and if it all depends on your bringing, alas! for the young child. This surely is a fundamental principle in all Christian education—the child is Christ's child. You have not to bring it *into*, but to bring it *up in* "the nurture and admonition of the Lord." You have to unfold to it the meaning and virtue of a relation that is, not to prepare it to enter into a relation which may be, or may not.

There is no need that I should repeat what I have said already of little children, whom Christ gathered in His arms, and blessed, and of whom He said, "*Suffer the little children to come unto Me, and forbid them not; for of such is the kingdom of heaven.*" It surely is significant that as the circle of the Church widened, and its members began to enter into the closest relations with the world around them, or were perplexed as to the effect of relations which they already sustained, the apostle Paul claims the children of *one* believing parent as holy. "*If any brother hath a wife that believeth not, and she be pleased to dwell with him, let him not put her away. And the woman which hath an husband that believeth not, and if he be pleased to dwell with her, let her not leave him. For the unbelieving husband is sanctified by the wife, and the unbelieving wife is sanctified by the husband: else were your children unclean; but now are they holy*" (1 Cor. vii. 12–14). And is there not a higher and more solemn sense in which Christ claims every human child as holy, not through the accident of a believing parent, but in virtue of that essential brotherhood which He has established with every infant of the human race?

To me, the word education would be meaningless, and the thing impossible, if there were not One who can come infinitely nearer to the child's heart than we can come, and bring influences infinitely more powerful than any that we can command, to bear upon his life. The first step, the vital step, in the work of education, is to bear witness to the child of Him. Not to talk to the child about Him as a Being outside and afar off, whom the child has to seek; before whom with due reverence he has to bend, and whose favourable audience he has to entreat. There is the grand mistake. We talk to children about Christ at a distance, far off in presence, far off in nature, far off in every way. We try to dilute our knowledge of Him to suit their little understandings, and to make familiar what in its own nature is remote and dread. But He is the light shining within them; He is present in all the little conflicts which are fought out in their childish hearts. Before they felt the touch of our magnet, the attraction of His was upon them. Before our voices wakened a familiar echo, His was pleading, wooing, winning, in the inner sanctuary of their young lives. There is a light of which every little child may be made conscious, shining in the darkness within it, and striving to conquer it; showing what is right in its little perplexities; teaching it that truth is better than lies, that love is better than hate, that peace is better than strife, and that right is better than wrong. This light gives to it the sensation of an inward glow like coming out into the sunlight, when it has done the right thing, or said the true word, at the cost of some effort, or by some little sacrifice ruled a temper or conquered a fault. Teach the child that that light is Christ, the Lord of the great universe, yet present with all His glorious power to guide the first thoughts, to train the first desires, and to take part in the first battles, in a young child's heart.

You have taken the first step, the divine step, in the education of your little one, when you have taught him to connect with Christ, and to recognise as the signs of His presence, every motion to good and every protest against evil, which rises up with a strength we little imagine in young children's souls. Let the child understand that the Lord of the universe is not afar off, watching its struggles, but within, stirring and sustaining them; and there will be a boldness in following the good and resisting the evil, which in these days, when we mainly believe in a far off Christ, we too constantly miss. *"Say not in thine heart, Who shall ascend into heaven? (that is, to bring Christ down from above:) or, Who shall descend into the deep? (that is, to bring up Christ again from the dead.)* .... *The word is nigh thee, even in thy mouth, and in thy heart,"* and in the mouth and in the heart of thy little one—the

Word "*Emmanuel,*" "God with us;" the engrafted Word, God within. We have not then to take the child to Christ, or to bring Christ to the child; we have to bear witness of a present Christ, with the child, within the child, in all the most familiar phenomena of its moral life.

And here is the sheet-anchor of a parent's hope. It is not that, if he strives, Christ will help him, but that Christ is already before him, and is the chief teacher; calling him to help in a work, which already engages the care and occupies the thought and the hand of God. Draw forth gently the latent consciousness of that as the first step in the higher education. Unfold to the child what these inward discords, these inward witnessings, strivings, yearnings, and aspirations mean. A good Lord and a destroyer struggling for the possession of his spirit; the one pleading and striving with infinite tenderness, the other ensnaring and enslaving with constant and malignant art. Kindle the thought of the high nature of this conflict, of which the daily tasks and rounds of life are to be the theatre; reveal, or rather teach the child to recognise, the presence of a form like unto the Son of man in the field of his conflict, the furnace of his trial.

Arm him, and send him forth into the battle, with the inspiring thought that he can never be alone in any extremity of peril, pain, or pressure; for, nearer to him than a mother, nearer than a brother, nearer than the most subtle tempter, nearer than the most hellish foe, is the Lord, who was within him from the beginning, and whose interest cannot be measured even by his own, in a free and noble unfolding of his life.

But there is a great danger here, against which it becomes Christian parents to be constantly on guard. It arises from the very earnestness of their desire to make their children the full sharers of the joy and the hope with which the gospel has lit their lives. It is a grievous mistake to let "the powers of the world to come" overshadow the young spirit too soon. As Moses put a veil over his face in speaking to his children, so God puts a veil over His face in speaking to every human child. That veil is the parent, who stands to the young child in "the stead of God;" happy for the parent, happy for the child, if he can fill for the time the place of God. The light should grow on the child's consciousness like the dawn, and the twilight is the parent's rule. There are parents who cannot be satisfied unless they flash the light at once in all its brightness on the young child's heart, and teach the little ones to mimic the functions and to touch the burdens which will one day try to the utmost their manly and womanly strength. The result of the process is, those ministering angels with the wings off, whom American writers first palmed upon us as human children; the vision of whom, could we see many of them about the pathways of life, would make the sad world sadder than it is. Happily, out of fiction, they are rare.

Those who rob us of the fun, the joyousness, the dash of childhood, can give us but poor equivalents in exchange. "Ministering children," early taught the gravity of a vocation, little know how they are killing manhood and womanhood, by robbing childhood of its buoyant and gleeful life; while children who catch early from a parent's contagious goodness and gentleness the love of ministry, are preparing to contribute something better than a wingless angel to the consolation and help of the world. It is a fatal mistake to press on a child's development, in order to force those early fruits, which are fair to look upon, but which quickly fade. A child's piety is one thing, a child's imitation of a man's or a woman's is another. I always tremble when I hear of those wondrously sage reflections and "good" actions, which Christian parents of a certain class delight to narrate. I fear lest the stem which bears such untimely buds should grow thin and sickly, and yield leaves only, when it should be bringing forth flowers and fruit. In a true Christian home, where the parents are taught of God, the parents' authority would long be to the child as the divine authority, and the dawn would brighten very slowly into the day. The time comes when the child begins to feel for some greater one behind the parent, and becomes conscious of the burdens and perplexities of life. Then let the parent produce his higher lessons, remembering always that it is as light, as life, as love, that the Lord reveals Himself to the soul and to the world. Were there more of this light and joy of the Lord in our Christian teaching, we might not have to mourn so constantly that the children of Christian households forsake Him, as though His names were darkness, terror, and death.

And well is it for us, in all our intercourse with and influence on our children, to remind ourselves, that there is One who holds their best interests yet dearer than we can hold them; and whose stake is yet more momentous than ours in the future of their life. He watches their every step with the most untiring vigilance, and shields their unguarded hours with the most jealous and tender care. He is nearer than their own thoughts to the spring of their actions, and haunts, as no man, no angel, no devil can haunt, the innermost sanctuary of their life. His love for them, His stake in them, His hope of them, has Calvary for its only measure; and He wields all the resources of divine power and wisdom to wrest them from the hand that would drag them to destruction, and to present them faultless, with us, in His own likeness, to His own eternal joy and triumph, in "the day of the manifestation of the sons of God."

VI.

THE NURTURE OF THE LORD.

"Bring them up in the nurture and admonition of the Lord."—EPH. vi. 4.

IN my last discourse I dwelt on the fundamental principle of a Christian education, the drawing forth and instructing the consciousness that Christ is with, is in, the child. Christ the light, an element of help, of joy; not as some parents systematically present Him, an element of gloom and dread. Let children know Him as the inspiration of their young efforts of duty, as their strength in their struggle against sin; as their sympathetic friend in all their dreary defeats and failures, nearer than their own consciousness to the springs of their thought and life. A Lord at hand and not afar off, within and not beneath or above; taking intimate and personal part in the action of their life drama, from the very dawnings of consciousness; witnessing, pleading, and striving, with boundless long-suffering within.

You have neither to take them to Christ nor to bring Christ to them. It may sound like a paradox, but I believe that the main reason why so many children of Christian households grow up inwardly ignorant of the Saviour, is that they have been so sedulously taught to seek Him. They should learn that He has sought them, and that He is there at the door of their hearts, yea, within the door, waiting only to be recognised and welcomed with love. The gospel is not, "Go forth to seek Christ and He will meet you." The words, "*Ask, and ye shall receive; seek, and ye shall find; knock, and the door shall be opened unto you,*" were spoken to men by One, who had come all the way from a heavenly throne that He might place Himself in their midst. He was seeking *them*, asking *them*, and knocking at the door of *their* hearts, that He might enter royally as of right and take up His abode. Tell them of a God who needs to be appeased, of a Saviour who waits to be moved to intercession, to plead the power of His blood on their behalf, and salvation is at once made to appear to them a hard, far off, and doubtful thing. We know nothing of a God needing to be appeased. We only hear of an atonement through the Lord who has made the atonement; we only hear of the need of reconciliation through a God who is reconciled; we only learn the value of intercession through a Saviour who is interceding, and who, while we were yet rebels, as careless of His love as the brutes, gave His life for us, that His intercession might have power to save.

If we would but begin with our children where God begins with us, it might go better with them. "*The word is nigh thee, in thy mouth and in thy heart.*" Look within. In the battle which is raging even in thy young heart, every high thought, every holy purpose, every heavenward aspiration, is the work of His love for thee; and every base thought, every impure passion, every worldly purpose, is the work of His enemy in thee, striving to pluck thee out of His hand. I think that this education of the consciousness to recognise the present Christ, the inward light that lighteth every man, and which shines very brightly in children's hearts, would lend dignity and energy to the moral struggle which begins with the first stirrings of freedom, and would wrest one mighty weapon of destruction out of the adversary's hand. There is nothing worse for the child than to feel that God is far off, and cannot care much about the battle of a young life; and that it matters little to Him or to any one what a child may think or do. It matters everything. From the first moment of consciousness the Lord has been with you, young soldier; learn to parade your soul before Him, and to answer to your name.

And to me this seems to be the only shield of the parent from what would else be a crushing burden of care. If we are to be at the main charge of this ministry, and if our influence is the chief educating power, then, as I have said, alas! for us, and alas! for the child. As Jesus bore witness of the Father, so we have to bear witness of the Saviour. If we bear witness of ourselves, of our private ideas of what a child should grow to be, our own image of goodness, purity, and truth, we may chance to see the little ones on whom we spend our wealth of effort growing into an image from which we shrink back with dread. I have seen it again and again. I have seen parents who had striven earnestly and with much self-denial to mould their children to an image which should satisfy their parental joy and pride, left in their old age to moan in bitterness of soul over the wreck of all their hopes. While little ones, trained early to recognise joyously the dawnings of a divine light and the stirrings of a divine life within, drawn out to realise their divine relations, and to cry with a child's frank heart, "Father, Father," in the ear of God, left free to unfold their native faculty and tendency under the eye and hand of a parent whose supreme concern was to know and to do His will, grow up in a fair and shapely adolescence, and into a maturity rich with noble and abundant fruit.

But what, upon this principle, is the true field of a parent's duty? If Christ is with the child, nearer than the parent, with power to reach the inner ear and to touch the inner springs, the parent's influence seems to fade into feebleness; it may help in some small measure, but it has no essential power. But it is the same with education as with everything else; man's power is that of the fellow-worker, the fellow-helper with God. In every field of human activity in which the higher human faculties find play, indeed in every region of activity, *the* power is of God. In every work, the essential power, the masculine power, is with Him. "It is the Lord thy God who giv-

7*

eth thee this power to get wealth." The intelligence, energy, and patience by which men win great successes, are ever fanned and kept at a white heat by the breath of God. In Him we *live*. If His breath kindles the flame of life, the glow passes swiftly through every pulse and organ, and energises them; if He withholds His inspiration they fail and die. As we rise into the higher spheres of work, the energising breath of God becomes more palpably the condition of all noble and fruitful activity. Moses, David, Isaiah, Paul, were from one point of view the most dependent thinkers and actors who have ever played their part in the theatre of history. "*And Moses said unto the Lord, O my Lord, I am not eloquent, neither heretofore, nor since Thou hast spoken unto Thy servant: but I am slow of speech, and of a slow tongue. And the Lord said unto him, Who hath made man's mouth? or who maketh the dumb, or deaf, or the seeing, or the blind? have not I the Lord? Now therefore go, and I will be with thy mouth, and teach thee what thou shalt say* (Exod. iv. 10–12).

"*And lest I should be exalted above measure through the abundance of the revelations, there was given to me a thorn in the flesh, the messen-*

ger of Satan to buffet me, lest I should be exalted above measure. For this thing I besought the Lord thrice, that it might depart from me. And He said unto me, My grace is sufficient for thee: for My strength is made perfect in weakness. Most gladly therefore will I rather glory in my infirmities, that the power of Christ may rest upon me. Therefore I take pleasure in infirmities, in reproaches, in necessities, in persecutions, in distresses, for Christ's sake: for when I am weak, then am I strong" (2 Cor. xii. 7–10).

"I am crucified with Christ: nevertheless I live; yet not I, but Christ liveth in me; and the life which I now live in the flesh, I live by the faith of the Son of God, who loved me, and gave Himself for me" (Gal. ii. 20).

"And ye shall be brought before governors and kings for My sake, for a testimony against them and the Gentiles. But when they deliver you up, take no thought how nor what ye shall speak; for it shall be given you in that same hour what ye shall speak. For it is not ye that speak, but the Spirit of your Father which speaketh in you" (Matt. x. 18–20).

And yet these were the very highest and freest expressions of human thought and will which the world has ever witnessed. No men have ever spoken so freely for God, yea, and to God, as these men who were completely dependent on His inspiration. None have acted so boldly, so grandly, in their human freedom, as those who took the suggestion of their every movement from the touch of His hand and the glance of His eye. And the reason is not difficult to discover. Man's nature moves in its fullest liberty, and touches the height of its possibilities, only when it is in perfect oneness with the mind and the will of God. The more completely God enters into it, the more nearly does it grow to the fulness of its native dignity and power. Man was made to be the fellow-worker with the Lord; the fellow-worker, as the woman works with man in the conduct of the home. "*The bride the Lamb's wife*," describes humanity under its highest possible conditions. Its freedom is the freedom which is possible in such union, the freedom of perfect sympathy and perfect love.

And thus the parents are Christ's co-workers in the nurture and culture of their little ones. It would be but partial truth to say that the supreme relation of the child is to Christ, and that the parent's influence is but a feather's weight in the scale. The parent's influence is part of Christ's influence; it is of His making and of His maintaining; and He is just robbed as it were of a vital organ, if a parent despises or even thinks lightly of this fellow-helping with Him. Throw yourself into the duty with all the zeal and energy which the thought of all that is hanging on your effort, for yourself, for your child, and for God, can inspire, and you will lend to the Master the most precious instrument that the universe could furnish for His work; while you may keep the instrument pure and keen, and meet for the Master's use, by remembering that your work is to bear witness for Him who is ever at work within, and to draw forth the child's consciousness that He is there. The more you believe in Christ's presence with your little one, the more, did you understand it rightly, would you feel your ministry to be essential to a true nurture and admonition in the Lord. The Lord is with *you*, as well as with your little one; and it is through you alone that He can complete His work. To this concert of spirit He is ever moving you. His zeal for your little one works through you as its chief organ. In truth, the Incarnation is a fact ever living, and it ever finds new manifestations.

God in man, man in God, is the key to the whole mystery of life.

I have said that nearer than all the tones and touches of the creation, far nearer, are the voices of the home. God is educating the child by all the objects with which He has surrounded it, drawing forth its apprehension, and widening its horizon. And He ever keeps objects on the dim bounds of that horizon to stimulate its effort. Whatever the child may see so as to know, God always cares that there shall be that which it faintly sees and hardly knows; so that a constant strain of effort is kept up, expanding and cultivating the powers. But man's influence is supreme. Nature cannot close the heart to man, but man may close the heart to nature. The passionate, spoilt child of a corrupt society, who pined "for a desert as his dwelling-place," that he might "all forget the human race," must have "one fair spirit for his minister." And it is ever thus. Man is and must be the supreme object to man. I doubt if affection so tender and so pure ever dwelt in human hearts, as that which the men who had cut themselves off from the world and its claims and loves, cherished towards the brethren of their monastery, to whom they knit their souls. Let these words of the wise and good Anselm, which he addressed to a brother monk, bear witness to the need which, even in the cloister, man has of man:—" Thou knewest how much I love thee, but I knew it not. He who has separated us has alone instructed me how dear to me thou wert. No, I knew not before the experience of thy absence how sweet it was to have thee, how bitter to have thee not. Thou hast another friend whom thou hast loved as much or more than me, to console thee, but I have no longer thee—thee! thee! thou understandest? and nothing to replace thee. Thou hast thy consolers, but I have only my wound. Those who rejoice in the possession of thee may perhaps be offended by what I say. Ah! let them content themselves with their joy, and permit me to weep for him whom I ever love."

Man must have man to cleave to; and from man all his highest directing and stimulating influences come. It is in the form of man that God claims the supreme rule over the world. And the home influence must inevitably be the dominant in the formation of character, or, where there is unusual native strength, in its direction and development. And there, too, it is chiefly settled whether it shall be a spring of joy or of bitterness to its possessor through life.

Many a noble gift, whose nobleness cannot be quite destroyed, even by the worst home influences, gets set so awry, or so poisoned in the springs, that it becomes mainly a sorrow to the man who is endowed with it, and to the world into which God sent it forth to be a benediction. Everything depends on the culture of the whole nature. You cannot cultivate a branch or a limb fairly, except through the trunk which bears it. If the whole nature is suffered to grow up warped, deformed, embittered, gifts, which might have traversed a wide orbit of blessing, become charged with a malignant energy, and live on, either as prodigies to startle, or as plagues to torment mankind. The home is mainly responsible for the *morale* of the men and women who are to carry on the development of society. And did I need any argument to strengthen the grounds of my belief in Him who has the world's destinies in a Father's charge, I should find it in the fact, that in spite of all that man does in human homes, in every generation, to poison human life in its very springs, there still *is* developement. Man holds on his path of progress; he goes from strength to strength led by an unseen hand, and triumphs over his own folly and weakness through the sustaining wisdom and energy of God.

I have dwelt at length on what seems to me to be the first step in all true education, the starting point of the higher life. The next step concerns the conscious relationship of the young child to Christ, the mystery of its moral nature, the experience of transgression, and its fruits, in an altered relation to the Father of Spirits, to man, and to the world. How, in a well-ordered Christian home, shall the parent deal with the question of sin? And here, as ever, the true course seems to be between two pernicious extremes. Let it alone, some say; why trouble the child with dark fancies, and teach it to see some dreadful evil in its little innocent half-conscious words and works? There is a school of philosophic religionists who would have us deal lightly with this whole question of sin. They believe that men are made ten times worse than they would otherwise be, by being tormented about their sins by the priests. Let them alone to the teaching of experience, they say; the burnt child dreads the fire; they will learn in time that the pleasure is not worth the pain, and live sober, peaceful, and sensible lives. This teaching of the priest, we are told, wakens a spirit of defiance; men sin the harder for it, and a bitter malignant temper gets possession of them. Treat transgression as having its origin mainly in ignorance, use wise discipline, sharp, if need be, to correct it; but be very careful not to cloud the bright heaven of a young child's life, by gloomy pictures of its moral condition and relations with the Supreme.

Thus one school argues. There are those, on the other hand, who think that the picture can hardly be painted black enough. They would have us impress upon the child a very vivid and terrible conviction of its sinful state, and of its peril if cut off, under the idea of driving it to Christ in the extremity of its agony, that it might be timely sheltered within His fold. Some of us have seen much of this method, and have marked its results. The child, being already within the fold of the Good Shepherd (and we may presume that those whom He gathered in His arms are not excluded from His fold), is in grave danger of being driven out of it again, by these terrible pictures of its condition, danger, and possible doom. "Teach them that they are sinners,—teach them that they are sinners,—teach them that they are sinners," reiterated a venerable and experienced minister once, as the first, second, and third head of a Christian education. And he had written a book on " Persuasives to Early Piety ! "

But I hold more with him than with the opposite party after all; if you understand, as I think that he did not understand, what the teaching means. You see the difference between teaching a child as a first lesson that he is a sinner, and watching earnestly for the fit occasion to unfold to him the nature and tendencies of that evil, the consciousness of which has become already developed within. We would keep the cloud out of the clear heaven of their young lives gladly enough, but, alas ! the devil is too busy. The cloud *will* gather, and *will* burst in a tempest, if we have not found the conductors which will carry its malign fire harmlessly away. We cannot afford to make light of transgression. There is that within the child which cannot make light of it. We may as well watch quietly a tumour gathering on his body, which will cripple him for life. Grapple with the thing we must, and with the reality of the thing. The fang is venomous, and unless we can neutralise the poison, the wound is death.

I think that I would not yield to the sternest theologian of the sternest school, in the firmness with which I hold two articles of his creed, that all that is good is of God, on the one hand, and that sin is the universal, deadly, damning mischief in man, on the other. Deal with it you must, and early; but again I plead, deal with it as the fellow-helper with God, watching His workings and interpreting them to the child. *You* have not to teach the child that he is a sinner; God has to teach it, and you have to watch His method and come in to His aid. If a young child, whose consciousness is but feebly cognizant of the mingled elements of which it is composed, be diligently taught to repeat that he is a sinner, and that God hates sin and must punish sin, then, as the intelligence developes, there can be but one result,—the child will grow up inevitably into distrust, and even dread of God. You may talk as you will of God's love, and of the gift of that love on Calvary, but the shock has been given, and the quiet trust and love, the bloom of a child's piety, has been destroyed.

Everything depends on the first image which

gets possession of the spirit, the first thought that lodges there. Is it to be Christ or sin? Let us watch God's method. If a child has been taught to recognise a light within, and has learnt that that light is Christ, and that Christ is love, the time will come, and come soon, when it will become conscious of a darkness—of something which does not love the light, and will not face the light —which stirs up a conflict and makes a confusion within—which fills the soul with pain, and sets it out of tune with life and with the world. Those are the seasons which a wise parent will watch for, to educate the consciousness of sin. There is an experience within, a work of God, which needs interpreting—a mystery, which the young soul is incompetent to solve. Words then have meanings. Sin, transgression, rebellion— yes, the soul knows full well what they mean. It longs to have them explained. It is ready to hear whence they spring, whom they wrong, and how they may be mastered and destroyed. Knowing Christ as the inner light, the first and chief Friend, the child is ready to harbour the thought of the grief with which sin afflicts Him, and to clasp the helping hand which He holds forth, that it may be saved. Let the field of the child's consciousness be bright with the light of the living Word, and every outburst of selfish greed or passion will show itself against that background black as night.

Ah! would we but study and follow the methods of God! Would we but wait until we see that He is teaching, and then help, as far as we may, these little ones to understand the lessons which He is impressing on their hearts!

The next step concerns the child and the written word. Alas! what a weary task-book the Bible is made in many an otherwise genial Christian home! When I see how all its diviner meanings are murdered, as children are taught to spell out of it, or trained to stand an examination in its facts and doctrines, in furtherance of what is understood to be " the religious element in education "—and if the angels are ever present as " the religious element " is being infused in schools, one would like to know what they think of it—I am again filled with amazement at the cordial faith in the Bible which survives the process. Though, if any are curious to discover the hotbed which forces, if not the root which generates, the most malignant unbelief, he may find it in what passes among us as the recognised process of religious education.

And the Bible suffers under this process in two ways. Its history is dealt with as if it were not history; and its truth as if it were dead and not vital truth. Its history gets studied mainly for its moral lessons, and the historic interest fades out of it. Surely it is more full of moral lessons than any history in the world; but this depends on the moral fulness of the life which it pourtrays. The moral lessons of any book may be measured by the largeness and vigour of the life which it sets forth; which if our writers of "tales with moral lessons," for children, would but remember, they would spare the poor young things which have to browse in their pastures much flatulent vacuity of mind and spirit, ending too often in entire incapacity for the higher business of life.

The Old Testament as history, and great part of it is history, is the most valuable ancient document in the world. The history of the free Jewish people—their struggle with the great oriental despotisms, and the power which, in virtue of a superior political and moral life, they were able to exert upon them even in captivity—is as rich in interest as the history of the free Grecian peoples, and their victorious struggle against the same despotisms at a later period of their development, or rather of their decay. And what is there in ancient literature comparable with the history of David? Where is the tale so rich in human interest, pathos, tenderness, courage, adventure, and brilliant achievement in policy and war? Children would read it gladly, and suck in its lessons as the glow of a summer noon, if we would leave them alone to pore over it as a history; and not cut it up into portions, and label them with morals, and do all that we can to persuade them that they are not to take the same enjoyment in it, that they take in any other ancient tale of brilliant and romantic life. It is grand and noble history, the whole historic Old Testament; and if we would but let our little ones bring their fresh young appetites to bear upon it, they would have that lodged within them which would unlock for them the inner meaning of all the histories which they may be called upon to study—the key, in a word, to the universal history of man.

The division into chapters and verses is admirably convenient for lessons, but is fatal to vital interest in the narratives. Nor do paragraph Bibles much mend the matter. The mischief is moral, and not mechanical; and this method of reading the Bible is so thoroughly wrought into us by long habit, that young minds are rather confused than helped by mere mechanical redistributions of the text. For I am not speaking altogether of the chapters and verses which the printer makes for us, but rather of the habit of piecing the work out into bits, each with a moral lesson to it, which good people carry about with them as prepared spiritual food; the teaching of which to their children, with the proper moral stimulus or sting appended, they regard as an essential element of the nurture and admonition of the Lord.

And when we come to the higher function of the Bible, the case is sadder still. Just as we will not wait for God to begin the teaching of young hearts about sin, so we will not wait for God to show to them the worth and the power of His word. We start at once by insisting on claims for it which it never urges for itself. Its absolute authority, its plenary inspiration, it never asserts; it leaves us to discover them as we discover the sun, and turn to it for light and fire.

The Bible, like the Master, speaks with authority, because so unlike the scribes; because the word spoken is so full of heavenly light and love, that men can see the Divine mark on it and rejoice. We do our very best to make the Bible speak *as* the scribes, who began by claiming authority, and demanded on that ground the acceptance of their truth. God asks no acceptance of His gifts but such as their worth may win for them. Oh! we of little faith, why cannot we trust His book to His own method, and let the light and the life with which He has freely charged it, glow and quicken through the world? What the Bible supremely wants is freedom. "You *must* think thus and thus about it, and about its every word," say the divines. "Leave it free to win its reverence," we answer; "there is light there bright enough to be seen without your glasses, and power enough to be only hampered with your officious hand."

And be sure that no amount of demonstration of its divine origin and authority, no reiteration of its claims, will win for it your child's homage. Formal reverence, such as men pay to scribes, you can compel, but true homage, mere authority never wins. The Bible is God's book to the child, precisely in the measure in which his sympathy is drawn forth to it, as presenting some outward image of his inner life. If he finds the key there which unlocks the wards of his experience; if he finds the truth there which casts a flood of light on the dark, and a dew of comfort on the sad passages of his life,—the Bible has found the child, not the child the Bible, and that finding never fails. If you can connect the outer word in the Book with the inner word in the life, and teach your child to seek it, not for formal lessons, not for knowledge of sacred things only, not for Sunday reading, but for real light in real darkness, real comfort in real sorrow, real help in real need,—you have made the Bible the man of his counsel until death. You have rendered his belief of the Bible absolutely proof against every effort of the adversary to undermine it. A thousand critics may assail its most sacred passages, it troubles him not; for him its light shines on, because it is God's light, unshorn of a single beam.

The last point on which I dwell is the education of the eye, and the whole seeing faculty of the child, to behold the wonderful works of God.

A great part, and a much neglected part of

the home education, concerns the faculties of observation, the drawing them out to apprehend the rich world of wonder and splendour which God has spread around even the basest beggar's child. A noted evangelical divine has recently been agitating the question, doubtfully and with the amount of wisdom to which popular preachers have accustomed us, whether it is worth while to study anything closely but the word of God, or what throws light on the word of God. Again I should be disposed to sympathise with his doubts, upon a true understanding of what the study of the divine word implies. The best way to blind ourselves to the sunlight is to stare at it; and the best way to miss the light which is in the divine word is to look at nothing else. To read nothing but the Bible and books about the Bible, is the surest way to stint its blessing. The Bible is larger than our faculties at their fullest expansion. The higher their culture, the wider their range of vision, the more of its truth they will be able to take in. In my small sphere, I am in the habit, as my congregation know very well, of studying each year some secular theme, some aspect of the creation, or some era of history, and bringing the results before them in a course of lectures on the subject. I call it secular, but to me it is most sacred. I do it distinctly that I may understand the Bible better, and be more fitted for my spiritual work; that I may know God's word and God himself more fully, by taking a wider view of what God has done in the material and human worlds. Never fear that the widest culture which you can give your children will imperil the supremacy of the word of God. If you have taught them the true secret of its value, and shown to them the true spring of its power, whatever stars of truth they may discover, their sun will never be eclipsed.

But teach them from the first to use their eyes and hands upon the world around them, for therefore was it sent. It exists for the education of these little ones, these nurselings of God, these infants of heaven. And our method is too often a shameful neglect of the riches and splendours of the universe, which God has flung round our daily paths with such royal and lavish hand. What are those glittering heavens telling nightly to the eager young eyes that search their star-sown depths, ignorant of their forms and motions, ignorant of those awful paths where the great Captain leads forth His flaming hosts by number, "and telleth them all by their names by the greatness of His might; and for that He is strong in power not one faileth?" Nor is the dust under our feet less rich in teaching, less full of the thoughts of God. The crystals of the dust are as wonderful as the constellations. Yet but one in a myriad has ever learnt their lore, pored over them till they revealed their secrets, and told as they *can* tell the struggles of their life. Teach your little ones to sing with the birds, and at matins; few know the glory of the dawn. Teach them to consider the lilies, how they grow, the mountains, how they uprear their thrones. Draw out the desire to observe and the power to observe the various phenomena of creation. It is like peopling the dull earth with living and unselfish friends.

I would have every child trained to take delight in some physical science of which observation is a leading function. I would have him taught to search out the thoughts of God in the creation, that "the trivial round, the common task," may unveil to him scenes of beauty and wonder, than which, may be, the angels see nought more wonderful and beautiful up there beyond the stars. I think that there must be scenes on earth of which those shining ones are joyful visitants; it was not of hasty and imperfect work, that God said "*behold it is very good.*" Every day the world seems to me more marvellously beautiful and more exquisitely wrought; and every day increases my sorrow that I learnt so little when I was young, and when the memory easily freights itself with treasures with which it never parts, about the stars, the clouds, the magnetic streams, the rocks, the mountains, the birds, the flowers, the music that floods the air, and the dust that I tread beneath my feet. Open the child's eye, as far as lies in your power, to take in the vision. The value of life is measured by the richness and variety of its experiences. Life ought to be worth double to your child what it has been worth to you. Your life ought to be his vantage ground, from which through the culture which God has strengthened you to give him, he may gather in the impressions of a far wider world.

Into the departments of education which fall under the charge of professional teachers, I do not feel competent to enter. One word only I will say. I should find it difficult to express the strength of my conviction of the value of a liberal education to a youth destined, like the majority of those whom I am addressing, to occupy his manhood with commercial pursuits. The study of the classical languages of antiquity, and the literature to which the mastery of the language opens the way, is incomparably the finest instrument of intellectual culture which is within our reach. Earnestly would I urge on every parent the duty of much effort and much self-denial to give his boy, yes and his girl too, some vision of that world. It is, like the history of Thucydides, as he himself describes it, "a possession for ever;" it adds something to the culture, which lifts the life into a higher sphere.

But prudent, practical parents are prone to question the use of this "dead" literature, and to insist on modern, and more immediately profitable themes. Perhaps its main value lies in the fact that it has no immediate and available use, and is, therefore, the finest instrument of a liberal education. A liberal education is that which considers the education, the drawing forth of the faculties, to be the main end of the discipline; while an illiberal education is that which asks for results capable of being put to immediate and profitable use. Most earnestly would I plead for a longer and larger measure of truly liberal culture, for the children who are to play their part on the busy stage of commercial life. It will give them a higher chance than you can easily imagine of lifting their life to a superior level, and making it worth tenfold to themselves and to the world. Believe that it will repay a hundredfold, whatever effort and denial it may cost.

Resolve that, God helping you, you will, at whatever sacrifice, bestow upon your children the gift of thoroughly disciplined and developed powers. Give them that, and take slight thought for the rest. Educate them, draw them out to their full stature physically, mentally, and spiritually; and then every farthing that you hoard for them is so much taken from the value of the priceless gift which you have bestowed. Lay up *in* them at any cost. It is the parents' honour and divine privilege to toil and suffer for the education of his child. Grudge nothing which that may cost you. Eternity only can reveal to you what it has been worth; and eternity only will reveal the curse of the hoards which the "rich in this world" lay up for their children, and the loss of noble effort and disciplined energy which this worse than idle provision has entailed. And eternity only will unfold to you how much of it has been laid up for the devil's storehouses; for thither, I am tempted to think, nine-tenths of the wealth that is hoarded for children finds its way at last.

VII.

RECREATION.

"To everything there is a season, and a time to every purpose under the heaven. A time to laugh . . . . . and a time to dance."—ECCLES. iii. 1, 4.

VARIETY is the key to the method of God in the management of our lives. Various influences, various objects, various experiences, various food. Man is continent of varieties. He can hold them clasped within his unity, and live by them. Rob him of variety, condemn him to monotony, in any department of his life, and you either madden or brutalise him. A rich variety of relations, scenes, and influences, is essential to the complete and healthy unfolding of his powers.

I suppose that there is no form of death more terrible than that which a man would suffer if he were fed to death on solid food. Fed to death! Yes; nothing is more easy. Let a man be shut up, and supplied with nothing but water and strong animal food; and, if he is kept to it long enough, he will die in horrible agonies, a loathsome, ghastly wreck. For a time, and for a special purpose—as when a man is in training for a contest—a regimen of strong animal food, with a minimum of those lighter elements which are regarded as the ornaments, but which in reality are very important features of a repast, may develope a remarkable amount of muscular fibre, and fit him to do the very utmost that under any conditions could be exacted of his frame. But if he were to keep up the regimen, month after month, and abstain from bread, vegetables, and fruit, the strong frame would wither, as if a hot blast had swept through it and dried up its vital juices. The joints and bands of the system would become relaxed, the limbs would move wearily; a dull, wearing, and ultimately agonising pain would seize them; the teeth would fall out of the gums, the eyes would strain out of the sockets, the features would wear an expression of intense and hopeless distress; and the man would either sink into a moping idiot, or die in insane despair.

It is now fully understood on all hands, that the lighter and more casual elements of our food are in their way quite as essential as the solid staple of it. If the one makes the fibre of the frame, the other makes the flesh—in which the fibre imbeds itself, and by which it carries on the play of life—fair, firm, and elastic. All force must be clothed to be fruitful; and the body, the flesh in which the muscular and nervous skeleton, so to speak, embosoms itself, is supplied mainly by the secondary elements of this food. They yield its juices, and give to it that mobility and play of power which make it a meet organ for a spirit's use. Let the body be robbed of these, and it becomes a mummy; for all the higher uses of a body—dead.

Transpose this into the moral key, and you have the history of what goes by the name of Puritanism. It is an effort, a very noble effort if you will, to live on too solid and stimulating food. For the moment, like a severe discipline when a man is in training, it nerved great men for great achievements. They cut themselves off from most of the invigorating and recreative juices which flow into a man from the glad, beautiful world around him, and up from the lily and the daisy beneath his feet. "*One thing I do,*" was their motto. Stars, lilies, the music of creation—

these are all distractions. "I have to wield 'the sword of the Lord and of Gideon,' in a battle of life or death against the devil and his works; and what time, what thought, have I to spare for dalliance with the lighter graces and ornaments of life?" There are some graceful words of Keble's, to which the ascetic spirit gives a certain tinge, which might present very fairly the image of their thought :—

> "Sweet is the smile of home; the mutual look
>   When hearts are of each other sure;
> Sweet all the joys that crowd the household nook,
>   The haunt of all affections pure.
>
> "Yet in the world even these abide, and we,
>   Above the world our calling boast:
> Once gain the mountain top, and thou art free;
>   Till then, who rest, presume; who turn to look, are lost."

One can fancy the spirit of these words nerving the hand of a stern Parliamentarian trooper, as he took a fresh grip of his sword-handle, and turned himself once more to the field where he meant to conquer or die. "*C'est magnifique, mais ce n'est pas la guerre,*" said the Frenchmen, when they saw the terrible cavalry charge at Balaclava. And we may say reverently of the Puritan, "It is magnificent, but it is not life." They lived only upon the strong meat of the word in its most concentrated form. It made them splendid men for the crisis—spare, stern, resolute, with moral muscles tough as wire; but in the long run Puritanism grew disjointed and dissolute; men maddened under its limitations and denials, and at length broke out into wild excesses. England had to pay the penalty of many a wanton and godless generation, for this effort to live only upon the solids of spiritual life.*

* I am conscious that I am using the word "Puritan" in a vague and popular way. It describes something to the popular apprehension which is very real, and which was characteristic of a great party which has left its mark very visibly on our national character and history. But strictly speaking, narrowness and want of geniality can by no means be fairly charged against the great Puritan leaders; nor, until it had become fanatical during its long and tremendous struggle, against the party which they led. I doubt if the world has ever seen such a rich and beautiful home life, as might be found in many a Puritan household in England during the early part of the seventeenth century. The most complete, cultivated, and courteous gentlemen, and the most sweet, lofty, and gracious women, that England has ever nurtured, were of that school. Able writers of our day, who by no means sympathise with our Nonconformist ideas, have been at pains to prove that we owe very much of that habit of thought and life which distinguishes the "English gentleman" (a species which is by itself in the world) to Puritan influence. And, certainly, a party which had Essex for its soldier, Selden for its lawyer, Vane for its statesman, and Milton for its poet, might lift up its head among the most cultivated and accomplished of the time. Nor was even Cromwell

The world, too, is as rich in varieties as the provision which God has made for the physical nourishment of man. There are nooks everywhere around us where nature is sporting, and simply enjoying herself. After large broad tracts, on which she has been working on a grand scale, and for high ends, you constantly discover a nook where she has manifestly had no end but beauty, and no care beyond the present joy. Every desert has its Elims, where the springs gurgle liquid music, and the palms fling cool shadow over the glowing sand. The tired pilgrim cannot choose but ungird himself, and fling himself lazily on the grass by the murmuring stream. Nature in such

without a rich vein of geniality, courtesy, and hearty appreciation of the graces and beauties of life. The evidence on this point is abundant. Take this little conversation with Whitlocke about the Swedish embassy, in proof:—" How could you pass over their long winter nights?" the Protector asked Whitlocke at the audience of return from his embassy. "I kept my people together," was the reply, "and in action and recreation, by having music in my house, and encouraging that and the exercise of dancing, which held them by the eyes and ears, and gave them diversion without any offence. And I caused the gentlemen to have disputations in Latin, and declamations upon words which I gave them." And the dialogue proceeded. *Cromwell*—" Those were very good diversions, and made your house a little academy." *Whitlocke*—"I thought these recreations better than gaming for money, or going forth to places of debauchery." *Cromwell*—" It was much better."

nooks is lavish of beauties; she makes a festa for her children, and will have them dance and sing. Dreary monotonies, weary marches along life's dusty levels, never fail to be broken at blessed intervals by stations where the very genius of the spot cries, "Rest a while and play." There are no long stretches of duty without green pastures here and there by the way, in which the jaded intellect and will may wander, unbound from the yoke a while, and recreate themselves for fresh toils.

Yet nature is not all dimpled with smiles. Stern motherly commandment is the broad expression of her countenance. "*In the sweat of thy brow shalt thou eat bread,*" is the sentence. God meant it, and nature means it, and is minded that you and I shall never forget it. But ever and anon, lest men faint by reason of the way, she bursts forth into such joyous merriment, that none but churls can escape the infection, and refuse to dance a measure with her before they pass on. But the heir of the old ascetic discipline may answer, "Yes, this is just the wantonness of nature. She is a Circe, and in these Elims and Hesperian gardens she ensnares and befools mankind. The Lord of nature has warned us against her seductions. Of all that comes to us so pleasantly and naturally we must beware. Our life is to be one long, stern struggle against the wooings and pressures of nature. We are to live here after a higher course than the course of this sin-tainted world which is around us, a course of which yon star is the symbol; and

> "Like as a star
> That maketh not haste,
> That taketh not rest,
>   Be each one fulfilling
> His God-given 'hest."

Thus the plea is set forth. I know not whether it was to rebuke this craven dread of nature, and of natural festivity, that Christ did His first great "sign" at a marriage festival, and on an element specially ministrant to the joy and exhilaration of the guests. It is as though He were resolved that their festivity should be hearty while they were about it; the best wine He brought forth to crown the feast. Was it to purge them of the fear of any of God's creatures, or of God's occasions of recreation; and to fill them with the fear lest evil passion and lustful licence should make unseemly the presence of the Lord?

But there are Christians living now, you may count them by myriads, who, were the Lord to reappear and to repeat this miracle, would shout at Him as they did of old, "Behold a gluttonous man and a winebibber, a friend of publicans and sinners!" Not that there is not very much in the facts of life to suggest the fear of which I have been speaking, if fear were the right entertainment of facts. But my belief is, that the fear to a great extent makes the facts, and is the real parent of the danger. How would the fear pass out of all gay hours and festive occasions, if we were conscious of the presence of Emmanuel in our midst! The danger is a real one, but we learn no immoderate pleasures from Nature. Would we but study and observe her order, instead of transgressing it, we should learn wisdom and temperance in her school. The danger is not to be mastered by the fear of Nature, but by the only fear which elevates and purifies—the fear of God.

The subject to which I am about to call your attention is recreation. By recreation I mean the play of the faculties, without any object beyond the immediate pleasure which the exercise of them yields. And let me insist on a first principle.

I. Play cannot in any wise, or by any one, be made the main business of life.

It is an element, an ingredient only, and it needs wise mixing. It is essentially a question of proportion, as it is with food, and this question of proportion is almost the main question of life. If a man attempts to live wholly upon the solids, his frame, as we have seen, becomes strained to the pitch of agony, and breaks in madness or death. If a man lives upon the slops, his frame passes quickly into pulp and flabbiness; the face becomes bleared, the expression vacant, the form gross, and the whole man vague, listless, and contemptible. And it is thus also with the moral man. The main food of man's higher life is work, hard, stern, uncompromising work. At least so the God who made us tells us in His book, and He presses home the lessons in forms from which it is impossible for us to escape. To work by fits and starts in the intervals of pleasure, to make that the main concern, and work the interlude, is to kill all pure enjoyment at the very heart. Work is the mother of rest, strain of pleasure.

No man knows what rest is but the weary; no man can enjoy but he who is relaxing a strain. The pleasures of idleness are like the smiles of an idiot, the very dreariest and ghastliest things under the sun. The men whose main business in life is to kill time, are killing much more than time, as they will discover in eternity.

Just as the lighter elements of food mingle with the more substantial in minor proportion—just as the nooks of violet-tinted shade spot here and there the broad hot fields where sinewy hands are reaping the corn—so in the same proportion must recreation temper our work. The idle know nothing of recreation, simply because they have nothing to recreate. He who dreams by the brook on a mossy bank through the hot summer's day, plashing its cool waters on his languid brow, and falling to dream again, may go home when he has done. Like Gideon's "ten thousand" who knelt by the stream, he will not be wanted. He who drinks of the brook by the way as he presses on, and he only, will "lift up the head." It is the true idea of recreation, a sipping of the brook by the way; its fruit cannot be better described than as a lifting up of the head.

II. Taking up, then, the broad idea of recreation, without attempting for the present a critical examination of its nature, my first plea on its behalf is for freedom.

By freedom I mean, the absence of artificial and unnatural circumscribing lines. I am not unmindful of the audience which I am addressing—for I preserve the form of spoken discourse advisedly in these pages—and I think it probable that most of those whom these words may reach will have been bred in a certain school, and with certain views as to recreation, derived from a noble spiritual ancestry, and the traditions of a stormy and struggling time. We Independents, who are the chief heirs of the ancient Nonconformist traditions, which stretch back into the early Puritan age and beyond, should speak and think with deep reverence of that narrowness of thought and sympathy, as we call it, which was characteristic of the great party (when it had settled into a party) from which we spring. We owe it mainly to that Nonconformity that we have a world at all in which we can decently dwell. The nature of the world against which the Puritans witnessed, and from which they sternly separated, is very imperfectly apprehended by most of us. It would amuse, if it did not sadden us, to hear simple-hearted lads and girls growing up amid the influences of a pious home, talking with grave face of separating themselves from the world—that is, a few innocent pursuits and enjoyments—under the idea that they are imitating the stern virtues of their ancestors, who cut themselves off from a world in which decent men and women could hardly live at all. It would be well though, if we took our traditions from the elders instead of the dregs of the school. The dread of amusement, the indifference to beauty, the determination somehow or other to make a dismal thing of life, which characterised the lees of the party embittered by a long struggle, we have taken for our inheritance; and till lately we thought it our duty to make the ashes conspicuous upon our heads as we passed along our path. There is much that is curious connected with this indifference to beauty in literature, architecture, and art generally, which has nothing specially to do with Puritan or even Roundhead times. St. Bernard might be supposed to be at the opposite pole to the Roundheads, who looked malignantly at the beauty of our cathedrals; or to our immediate forefathers, who thought to honour with the sternest simplicity, or the barest ugliness of form, the spiritual use of their meeting-houses, which, happily, the exigencies of the time compelled them to keep carefully out of sight. But Bernard might have been a Roundhead preacher, taking up his testimony against the architectural harlotry of King's College Chapel or Wells Cathedral, or even a stiff Independent, bearing witness against the milder beauties of such Gothic as we allow ourselves in these days, when he exclaims,

"O vanity of vanities! but not more vain than foolish. The Church's walls are resplendent, but the poor are not there. . . . . . . The curious find wherewith to amuse themselves—the wretched find no stay for them in their misery. Why, at least, do we not reverence the images of the saints, with which the very pavement we walk on is covered. Often an angel's mouth we spit into, and the face of some saint trodden on by the passers-by. . . . . . But if we cannot do without the images, why can we not spare the brilliant colours? What has all this to do with monks, with professors of poverty, with men of spiritual minds? Again, in the cloisters, what is the meaning of those ridiculous monsters, of that deformed beauty, that beautiful deformity, before the very eyes of the brethren when reading? What are disgusting monkeys there for, or ferocious lions, or horrible centaurs, or spotted tigers, or fighting soldiers, or huntsmen sounding the bugle? You may see there one head with many bodies, or one body with numerous heads. Here is a quadruped with a serpent's tail; there is a fish with a beast's head; there is a creature, in front of a horse, behind a goat; another has horns at one end, and a horse's tail at the other. In fact, such an endless variety of forms appear everywhere, that it is more pleasant to read in the stonework than in books, and to spend the day in admiring these oddities, than in meditating on the law of God. Good God! if we are not ashamed of these absurdities, why do not we grieve at the cost of them?—Morison's *St. Bernard*, p. 148.

Mr. Morison quotes in a note an amusing but very suggestive passage from Mr. Carlyle's Latter-day Pamphlets, which is not without its bearings on the matter in hand.

"'May the devil fly away with the fine arts,' exclaimed confidentially once in my hearing, one of our most distinguished public men; a sentiment that often recurs to me. I perceive too well how true it is in our case. A public man, intent on any real business, does, I suppose, find the fine arts rather imaginary, ... feels them to be a pretentious nothingness; a confused superfluity and nuisance, purchased with cost; what he, in brief language, denominates a bore."

But I am wandering from my theme. Art is not in question here, but recreation. Art, as recreative, is a matter on which I may have a word to say by and by. I plead for freedom of recreation—the absence of artificial and unnatural limitations. And I write specially for those whose lot in life subjects them to these limitations, and for the parents who impose them, and who hold to what they mistake for the old traditions in these matters, together with much that is very noble and very beautiful in their homes. And for these Christian homes, for their simplicity and health, for the manliness and the womanliness of the youths and maidens who are to go forth from them, I am persuaded that a chief necessity is freedom. I believe that the time is come when those who are looked to for teaching must speak out about this, wisely and temperately on the one hand, but clearly and firmly on the other.

The fundamental idea of the discipline of

such Christian homes seems to be, that "professing" Christians must draw a formal line between their pursuits and pleasures, and the pursuits and pleasures of what is called the world, or their "profession" will become "*vox et prætera nihil.*" I hold this idea to be a radically false one. Christ did nothing of the kind, and He taught His disciples to do nothing of the kind. He went, and His disciples went, freely about the world, not drawing a line, but living a life which condemned the evil which was in the world, and justified the good. *We* have taken to lines and forgotten lives. It is time that we began anew. We are living upon the negations and abstinences of our fathers. Lines drew *themselves* in the days when the host at every great dinner party who did not do his best to intoxicate his guests, was held to be churlish; when the theatre was the open and shameless haunt of the most bedizened prostitutes in the town, and when the man who touched a card or a cue was in a fair way to be tempted to gamble away his fortune. Lines drew themselves in those days for every pure-hearted self-respectful Christian; and it is just because our fathers had the firmness to keep within the lines which drew themselves so clearly, and to protest by their lives against the doings without them, that we live in days in which the lines have happily become dim. This tradition of limits survives, but we are puzzled to know where to place them; and so we defend the old ones with what appearance of earnestness we may. "Men, after all, are pretty much like sheep," as Richter says; "if you meet a flock of sheep coming along a lane, and put your stick against the wall, the first sheep will jump over it, but if you take your stick away, all the others will jump too."

I am persuaded that the mental and moral health of our children is grievously impaired by the miserably unreal distinctions which we draw between things which may be allowed and things which may not. "The line must be drawn somewhere," seems to be our fundamental thesis. And so we occupy ourselves with barriers, instead of nourishing an intelligent and manly habit of discernment in ourselves and in our children, and leaving the lines as we go about the world to be determined by the shadow which is cast by our lives. Take a homely specimen. At a time when French wines were not so common and cheap as happily they are now, a good deacon of one of our churches was sadly scandalised at seeing some of the costly and luxurious beverage at the table of a brother deacon with whom he was dining. On being pressed for the reason of his discomfortable aspect, he could only plead, "Well, you know, you must draw the line somewhere—I draw mine at port."

It sounds absurd; but those who laugh are doing precisely the same things in principle every day. There are certain amusements, which those whom we choose to call people of the world indulge in—a game of cards, a game of billiards, a play now and then, or what you will—which our stricter habit, learnt, as I have said, from a goodly ancestry, places under a ban. But the wonderful part of the matter is here. You will find in Christian homes, and in the habits of Christian society, not exactly the same things, but imitations of them on a small scale, which come as near to them as possible. There are very few of the world's honest amusements—and by honest I mean such as are not vicious in their essence or in their palpable associations—which are not issued in smaller type for the amusement of "professing Christians" and their children. We get as near to the line as possible, and press against it—but "we must draw the line somewhere" still.

There are entertainments in London—excellent, I dare say—to which Christian people throng with their children, which lack nothing of the theatre but the genius and the name. There are pious little books issued by the myriad—I wish I could call them excellent too, but the major part of such as I have come across seem to me the sickliest trash, with as much taste as the white of an egg—which are meant to supply the craving of hungry young souls for honest fairy tales and the like, to their utter damage and loss. Fairy tales are a charming condiment in the intellectual food of children; they help to keep alive the sense of the infinite beauty and wonderfulness of the world, which "good little books," even when they are didactically trying to describe it, drearily deny. And, turn where you will, you find Christian recreation provided after the pattern of worldly recreation, with some slight moral infusions in it, or some puling application, which is supposed to keep it within the line. How strangely careless God must have been, all these ages, of the moral and intellectual culture of "these little ones," if our modern method is the right one: for nothing wearing its likeness is to be found in His works or in His word! There are tales enough in His book with the moral *in* them, not after them; and no visions of fairy-land which the most cunning playwright has conjured out of his teeming brain, can mate that world of wonder and splendour which He has unveiled to us in His Apocalypse.

But, be that as it may, it appears to me to be most detrimental to the moral nurture of your children, that they should be allowed to think, that you press as near to the line as you dare, and that there is a hankering, though restrained by principle, for that which lies beyond. They are more likely to catch the infection of the hankering than of the restraint. And it generally happens that the form of amusement which is allowed in "strict families," while following "the world" up to a certain point, stops short where the real power of recreation—that is, the power of giving a joyful play to the faculties— begins. It is recreation and water, and that so weak, that all stimulating, re-invigorating power is lost. In fact, looking around on those poor imitations of the recreations of the world which we allow ourselves and our children to enjoy, I am driven to the conclusion, that we have not made our proscription of the great recreative influences, towards which man's nature has yearned in all ages—the drama and the dance, for instance—anything like a success. We simply drop down into feeble and timid forms of them, and do with a half heart and a restless conscience, what must be done with a whole heart and a good conscience, if it is to have any virtue in it at all.

The reasons of moderation, the persuasives to self-control, are one thing; they have to do with what is noblest in us. The "touch not, taste not, handle not" method is another thing, and has to do with what is selfish, narrow, and base. Unless there be broad reasons, such as the eye of a healthy moral sense gathers at once, for the commandment, the proscription of this or that place, exercise, or pursuit, robs your children of the noblest moral discipline of their youth—the exercise of temperance and self-control. It is an easier method than the divine, this method of "forbidding." It is easily taught, easily learnt, and it yields for the moment a wonderful appearance of success. But the restraint that is learnt in freedom is the only restraint that has any living force in it. It is a longer and a harder matter to learn it; but it forms a fortress whose strength is something nobler than the absence of an assailant; it holds its own against all comers, and remains impregnable through eternity.

We are widening our views about all other matters. Ten years ago it was thought heresy to utter truths, which now we hear gladly that every one believes. We have larger, freer thoughts about our divine relations, about the Bible, about life's meaning and duties, and it is time that we enlarged our thoughts about our recreations. It is time that we ceased our proscriptions of what nature yearns for, and the effort to hedge about young steps with unnatural and artificial lines. Let us throw our whole strength into the cultivation of that noble moderation and self-restraint which was the true glory and dignity of Puritan homes. That is the grand safeguard. That fortress is safe whose firm defenders are ever within. It is the noblest and most precious fruit of education—of difficult culture if of high virtue; but no Christian parent may dare to shrink from the task. *Men* shrink from freedom as the mother of licence. *Christ* had no dread of it when He sent "*the perfect law of liberty*" into the world. The real mother of licence is restriction and exclusion. None plunge so madly into pleasures, as those who have been fretted through youth by unnatural restraints.* You do not keep your children out of the natural and honest pleasures of young life by your lines and hedges, you simply send them into them with an untrained will and a trembling conscience. They have no belief that the Lord can be there. Of that belief you have robbed them; and, robbed of that belief, the devil makes sport and spoil of them at his will.

III. I now pass on to consider the essential idea of recreation, which I have defined already as the free play and exercise of the powers, for the pure sake of the pleasure which it affords.

The end is to recreate, to make anew—as nature comes forth each day from her bath of dews, and man from his bath of rest. Nature is recreated each morning. Each sunrise, in glittering beauty, as, on the first morning of creation, she sings, with pure, fresh, virgin voice, her matin song to God. There is song in the morning wind among the boughs; there is music as the mountain mists draw off their embattled squadrons, and leave the jocund day the master of the field. The floods of splendour which stream upon the air are vocal with praises, which yon lark, bathed in the golden glory, is rehearsing at the gate of heaven. Nature "shouts for joy" at morning prime, "she also sings." And the end of recreation is to make us sing instead of moaning at our tasks. It is to restore the tension of the spring of power, and to make work an exhilarating exercise instead of a heart-breaking toil. Life is a race, a battle, a stretching on to an end. The tension is too keen for pleasure—the Eden-life is over. If the strain is never relaxed it becomes sharp agony, and fills the air with moans. So God bids us unbind the yoke awhile and play.

Rest is not recreation. If a man is so worn out by toil that, like a tired-out horse, he just drops when he is unyoked, and lies slumbering until he is yoked again, he is not recreating. No new joy will come to such a man in his work; mere rest never made any man dance and sing. The only recreation is in the free and joyous play of the powers, for the sake of the pure pleasure which the exercise yields. A bright walk in the summer evening through the meadows in the sunset glow, a bath in the dewy evening air filled with a golden glory, while the hum of life settles down to its repose—here is something which belongs to us, and which God enables us by a thousand senses to take in. Every sense is athrill with delight as it exercises itself on the objects with which God has surrounded it in creation, and has drunk in a full draught of joy from an unfailing spring. The recreation has renewed us; we go back with new and joyful energy to our tasks. And he who, when his work is done, has entered into the keen rivalry of athletic games and sports, and has strained his muscles for no compulsion but his "own sweet will" to strain them, goes home weary in limb, but refreshed and recreated in spirit, and something of the joy of his game abides with him and sings through his work. Another turns from the weary day-book and ledger to read with instructed eye a page out of the great Book of the Creation; he spends his evening in his laboratory watching the play of the electric fire, or the rudiments of things taking their crystal forms under his hand, and pores over it, all out of pure love, with an ever-fresh wonder and delight. The morning will call him forth with new energy to his business occupations, he will go forth from his home a new-made man to his daily tasks. Another finds his delight in the keen play of intellect, the quick flashing glances of sympathy, in music and the music of motion, and all the relaxations and recreations of home-life and society.

Happiest, perhaps, are those whose taste and culture enable them to find a rich recreation in the pursuits and enjoyments of art. The habit of studying the Divine handiwork, to discover its order and method, that we may think over again the great thoughts of God, and cultivate our powers to express them by means which our own nature supplies, affords the highest and purest recreation which is possible for man. It unveils to us the mystery of the creation, and gives to us the loftiest fellowship with our friends. Those able to practise little, may at any rate train themselves to judge and enjoy. The pleasure thus yielded will be the more purely recreative, in that it is so far removed from the scenes and influences of the daily toils. Music, the fine arts, and the higher forms of literature, call unused faculties into play, and increase immensely both the capacity of the nature and the interest and enjoyment of life. Higher uses of the powers thus cultivated we shall discover, when the things " which eye hath not seen, which ear hath not heard, and which it hath not entered into the heart of man to conceive," shall appear. The essence of the recreation in all cases is the joy which is found in the exercise of the powers, under no constraint but that of the pleasure which the exercise yields. It is a draught by the way from the pure fountain of life's pleasure, which sin sealed up in Eden, and which Christ will unseal for ever in Heaven. It comes, or it ought to come, if we but knew what recreation meant, to throw some cheer into our daily tasks, and to remind us of a sphere for which those daily tasks are training us, where the free play of our powers will be a perennial bliss. It should give us a snatch of song to lighten our labours; a breath of cool fresh air to play through the heated work-room of life. Nothing is recreation which does not tend to renew the spring, whatever else it may be. Recreation is emphatically a taste of the lost joy which was once man's heritage in Eden; the hard stern toil of life, under the sentence, "In the sweat of thy brow shalt thou eat bread," is the condition of our regaining it, if we are found faithful, in heaven. By this, test your recreations. All else, instead of recreating, dissipates the powers.

But why limit such recreation? It is noble and beautiful, and why should it not occupy all our time and power? Surely it would roll back the curse from us. Why should we "fardels bear, and grunt and sweat under a weary life," when recreation such as would give joyful play to all our faculties lies so near to our hand? Let us work while we must, and recreate just as much and as often as we can. Alas! the curse is within, as well as on our lot; if that may be called a curse which brings such boundless blessing in its train. The law of labour is in *us*, as well as on our world. There is no escape from the necessity but by missing a benediction. The daily bread of our life is labour. The body can as well live without bread as the mind and spirit without work. The sentence of toil is not rolled back from us, nor will it be rolled back until our powers are so developed, that their easy joyous play will be more productive than now our most consuming toil. The mere play of a man of Turner's power is worth more, and will produce more, than the most elaborate efforts of a genius of meaner strain. And his power grew by such labour as few men in his generation, busy as it was, could mate.

Heaven is educating us all for a great future; and the full strain of work is the condition of our recreating to some high purpose in time. Certain it is that recreation degenerates swiftly into dissipation, unless it comes as the interlude to long, hard spells of work. Man cannot make recreation his business, without poisoning its very springs, and becoming that saddest of all objects to look upon, a man with no business in the world. Our business here is to work, to work with unflagging energy. Recreation is to be the handmaid of toil here, and to supersede toil in eternity.

I must say a word in concluding these remarks, on the perils of recreation, the directions in which it runs very easily into excess.

The worst—though, from another point of view, we might call it the best—of Englishmen is, the intense energy which they throw into all their pursuits. Wherever you find them in earnest, they throw off all moderation, and manifest a fierce energy which is wonderful and sometimes terrible to behold. But my business is with recreation now. Foreigners think that we do not understand it, we seem so intensely in earnest about it; and some Englishmen, who have their eyes open, are beginning to fear that much of the geniality and joy of life is being killed by the new habits of the times. One does not meet with so much of the racy humour which used to be so characteristic of us; and all the qualities which flourish best in quiet nooks of life are becoming year by year more rare. And I sometimes fear that our great national games are going the same way to death. Our physical recreations, which are the simplest and most invigorating, are fast losing their recreative power. We are spending on our play an amount of energy and endurance which we can afford only for our tasks. Athletic sports have passed under the sway of competition, and our most splendid young athletes will carry crippled and exhausted bodies into the arena of life as the result. Even cricket, our grand old English game, has become a battle, and just in that measure it has ceased to be a play. When men have to pad themselves in the most uncouth and awkward guise before they handle the bat, and stand up to their wickets at the peril of a blow which may easily cripple them for life, the sport passes out of the game. It becomes a battle—a fine one, if you will—which you may watch with the keenest interest; but it is really a business, and it passes into the hands of the men who can make it the study of their lives. There may be the highest skill, but there is little fun, in playing a ball flung with the force of a catapult, with a fair prospect of a broken ankle-bone if you miss it. The excitement is too high and grave for pleasure, and the refreshment of a game of cricket is becoming a thing of the past.

Athletic sports at our universities and in our rifle regiments develope a marvellous pluck and power in our young gymnasts, but they take altogether too much out of them just when their frames are setting; and when we want them for the nobler and more serious work of life, how many of them will be mere wrecks! One wishes that a list could be drawn up of the number of fine lads who are disabled for life by rowing, running, and jumping matches, every year, simply through having been put under a too prolonged and oppressive strain. I believe that the Oxford and Cambridge middle-class examinations are working much mischief in the same direction. There can be no question that they have given a very strong stimulus to education, mainly through acting on the educators. But the young lads who are subjected to all the strain and excitement of a public competition, just when they want all their nervous force to develope their constitution, have many of them to pay a heavy compensation when they go forth into life. We have just strung the instrument up to its fullest tension in every string. It is all eager, intense, and exhaustive toil; and we shall have the strings cracking, and the whole tone of our constitution as a people lowered.

And to pass for a moment to another sphere of recreation. Do you think that the Psalmists could have written about dancing as they did, if they had been shut up till four o'clock in the morning in the miseries of a modern ball-room, choked by the gas-poisoned atmosphere, and with their clothes almost torn off their backs in the supper-room crush? What we want imperatively is, not new abstinences, but new moderations—the resolution running through society that recreation shall be recreative, and shall send men and women back, not expended, but invigorated and gladdened, to their work. We do our very best to turn our recreations into dissipations, by length of time and elaborate accessories. Concerts, theatres, dances, sports, all suffer miserably from the same disease—excess. All true recreation will be brief, simple, and ready to hand.

I have spoken of dissipation; it is the precise opposite of recreation—the one gathers and stores, the other scatters and squanders, power. Much dissipation is simply recreation in excess—the recreation of men who are too hard-worked, or too ill-trained, to enjoy any but the most fiery stimulant by way of change. Over-long hours, over-hard strain, drive men to dissipation, instead of recreation, for the alternative which they need. Foul homes, hot work-shops, and bad food, are the great nurses of dram-drinking. Our social system and social state are answerable for a fearful amount of that drunkenness which is our national curse and shame. Dissipation in any form is the great drain of life. Life is the most precious thing which God has given or can give us. What shall a man give in exchange for his life? You have only a certain amount in you of life. You may spend it quickly or slowly. You may expend or husband it; but when it is gone, there is an end. No agony of effort or prayer can bring you a new store.

"A short life and a merry one" is the cry of dissipation. "A noble life and an eternal one" is the creed of the man who has learned the secret of life from God. "A short life and a merry one!" Merry! I wish you could come in upon your merry life for a moment, fresh and pure from some higher region, and see its ghastly guise. Merry! May I be out of the hearing of your merriment, when you come forth sick, pallid, blear-eyed, and, as you say, "shaky," from your night's debauch; and may God keep me from hearing you moan when the brief debauch of life is over, and you sink down, a fetid, wailing mass of corruption, into the pit which burns all the waste of the universe for ever.

Recreate with Christ in presence. He is as glad with us at our marriage festivals, yea, even at our sports and pastimes, as He is sad with us by our dear ones' graves. Learn from Him the secret of moderation, of wise temperance, of strong self-control. Seek strength from Him to make covenants with yourself, and keep them; it lies at the root of all noble living, and it is learned only in the free school of God.

VIII.

GETTING OUT INTO LIFE.

"*And Isaac sent away Jacob.*"—GEN. xxviii. 5.

BITTER sweet is the cup of life. Sweetness as of paradise, bitterness as of death. Intenser joy than is known to mortals no creature knoweth, but alternate with intenser pain. I heard two poor men the other day, in a railway carriage, narrating to each other their experiences; they seemed to have had a long, stern struggle. "It is a hard life," said one; "I reckon we earn our bite and sup at any rate." "Yes," I thought, "we do; and some of us, if we cannot earn, try hard to win something more, the bread of the love and sympathy of God."

For those who are finely strung, and whose inner chords vibrate keenly to the lightest touch, it is stern work to live. How many men and women are there living upon earth at this moment who, were the simple question, "To be or not to be?" set before them with no dread shapes there in the shadows, would lie down full joyfully to rest in the cold bed of death? Parents know the sweetness and bitterness in the fullest measure. No cry so glad has ever been heard on earth as that first outburst of a mother's joy and triumph, "*I have gotten a man, the Lord!*" no moan but one, so bitter, so desolate, has ever wailed through the night as that cry of a father's breaking heart, "*O my son Absalom! my son, my son Absalom. Would God I had died for thee, O Absalom, my son, my son!*" There are those who will read these lines who have known both the bitterness and sweetness in a measure, who have tasted a joy such as an angel might stoop to share with them, and have known an agony which they were tempted to think, as they writhed under it, could be mated only among the fiends.

But no; it is not to the infernal spheres that we are driven, to understand such a cry as David's. Blessed be God, the joy and the sorrow, the sweetness and the bitterness, are seen, both within the circle of His own life. He, serene in His eternal blessedness, as we delight to picture Him, has tasted Himself both a joy and an anguish of which ours are but the shadows. The whole key to our experience, as far as it arises out of what is inevitable in life, is to be found in God. There is its explanation, there is its justification, and there, if we rejoice purely and suffer bravely, is its essential glory. We may not shudder, we may not even shrink, when the gloom gathers over us; we are but rising into a divine experience, and becoming capable of the most intimate fellowship with God.

The home-life is the sphere of the most intense of human experiences. It is life in the keenest tension and to the loftiest strain. But I must again recall to you a principle which I have already dwelt upon, that the home-life gives the key-note to all life, and that all who do not shut their hearts to human sympathy and emotion, in some measure share its experience and taste its cup. For all love is the same love. Love of wife, love of child, love of friend, love of man, to the great paternal natures who can gather a wide company of Christ's poor brethren to their embrace, are all the same love, one in their fountain, diverse only in their currents, and not other than the love of God. And he who has the heart to love has the heart to live, and the heart to suffer.

There is that in him, though to the eye he may live mainly solitary, which explains to him all a parent's joys and sorrows, and gives him a knowledge of what is very deep in the life of God. None who have not denied the human, can turn a deaf ear when the experience of loving hearts is pictured; they know both the delight and the anguish in their measure, and can enter into the inner sanctuary of life.

But the full experience the parent alone can know, and those who have taken willingly a parent's burden on their hearts. I have seen brave and patient women crushed down into speechless agony by the dying struggles, or worse, by the shame of their cherished ones; and I have seen, too, a proud joy in parents' eyes, which it were worth the peril of the anguish to taste. Oh, children, children! God has set you for the fall and the rising again of the life-springs in those who nurture you; yea, a sword shall pierce the heart of her that gave you birth. Happy the child who has never cost father or mother the sharpest pang that has ever pierced them. Little dream you, in your young buoyant carelessness, how the hearts are quivering with whose strings you wantonly play, how the hopes throb and thrill which you daily lift or lower. The sorrows begin early. "*I will greatly multiply thy sorrow and thy conception.*" In pain the little ones are brought forth; in pain and care they are nurtured. Nothing is more wonderful than the measure of sorrow with which all that touches our highest joys is brought into the world. Nay, the little ones begin to taste it from the first; it is not long before their eyes fill with tears, and their voice sobs with pain. And it is just this pain of a little helpless infant which is so hard to comprehend, and so bitter to bear. "*In sorrow shalt thou bring forth children*"—and in sorrow shall they be reared.

But the joys and the sorrows cluster most thickly around the era of the home life which we have now to contemplate, when the children, full-grown, must go forth into the world. If one were in any need of considerations to strengthen the conviction, that the moral is the supreme element in the human constitution, one might find it in the fact, that all the cares, joys, and sorrows of a parent deepen quite infinitely when the child is growing to manhood or womanhood, and is stretching out a hand to grasp at the reins of life. There is nothing which the *young* child can do or suffer which touches us to the quick. The solemn endowment of man lies there enfolded, as the petals within the sheath of the bud; and as it unfolds something solemn passes out of it into the relations of the home. We enter as parents into a new world of experience, when the knowledge of good and evil is fully developed in our little ones; and as they grow to maturity, and pass more and more out of the charmed circle in which they are sheltered by our shield, the care deepens, and casts a shadow over our lives. Honour and shame, blessing and cursing, heaven and hell, then loom in sight. The young life so dear to us goes forth from the land-locked harbour of our love, to be tossed on a stormy ocean, with dread perils all around, and wrecks not a few scattered on the shore.

"*And Isaac sent away Jacob.*" The time had come; why or how in that special instance we need not stay to inquire. The time does come in all homes when the household must bud like the polyp, and develope into new households, and prepare to occupy new lands of promise. Life stirs in the bud joyously; but the old stem groans and shudders as the young things part. There is the glowing and thrilling life of spring in the young ones; there is power astir in them which can make a summer; "*they shout for joy, they also sing.*" But the old stock has the chill of the coming winter in it, and when the sons and daughters are sent forth, the winter comes swiftly on. "*Isaac sent away Jacob.*" The patriarch of all the families of the earth, he looms there in the misty morning twilight, a grand and stately form. He sends forth his son, as a thousand generations have sent forth theirs, with straining eyes and aching hearts, as they watched them vanish. Once again he saw his Jacob, when his eyes were dim and his step tottering; but the mother never again folded her darling to her heart. "*Now therefore, my son, obey my voice; and arise, flee thou to Laban my brother, to Haran; and tarry there a few days, until thy brother's fury turn away. Until thy brother's anger turn away from thee, and he forget that which thou hast done unto him; then will I send and fetch thee from thence.*" She paid the bitter penalty of her craft. She won the birthright; she lost the child. So Isaac sent him forth.

And that little prattler, weaving her fairy chain of charms around your heart-strings, will one day go forth weeping, but with a bride's proud joy shining through her tears. That brave boy, whose merry laugh has been ringing through your home, whose studies you have watched, whose sports you have shared, whose promise you have marked with fond exultation, will go forth one day like Jacob, it may be to the far East like him, and leave you bare, stript like the tree of autumn; strong and stately yet, but bare, bare for ever, were it not for the promise of the eternal spring. But for this promise, but for the hope of the world where the family will meet again, to break up no more for ever, I often think that the silent childless home of the old people, when the young ones are gone out into life, would be one of the saddest things under the sun. The echoes of loved and familiar voices silent, the notes of the sweetest music that a parent's ear can listen to, quite still.

But the getting them out is, after all, the great work, the great care of a parent's life. To this end all his efforts and toils are directed; and when this end is gained, he is ready to say with Simeon, "*Lord, now lettest Thou Thy servant depart in peace*," "my work here is done." But new joys will spring if he is but patient. Little ones will gather again around his knees, of whom the joy is his, but not the burden. Still, something is lost which in this world he will never recover. Children's children can never quite supply the place of our own, for the very care and burden of the nurture of children enriches life. The joys of old age are set on the whole in a lower key, as the westering sun loses something of his mid-day fire. But it has no need to be cheerless or joyless; while its gathering shadows are lit to the eye of faith by a solemn and holy lustre, which streams from the fountain of eternal sunlight, the dawn of that day which shall break on the spirit as the body settles into the night of death.

"Getting out into life," or "getting young people out into life." They are peculiar terms, though quite familiar, and their meaning reaches farther than appears. Next to the birth of the infant, the settling of the youth or maiden in life is the great transaction of the home. Indeed, it is a kind of second birth to them, a birth into a wider world. It is a time of sore anxiety, and often of dire perplexity. The whole future of a human life seems to be hanging on your decision—a decision which may either nurse it to a noble fruitfulness, or blight it to a premature decay. It seems to be a matter of vital importance for you to discover the exact work, or the exact sphere, for which your son or daughter may be most fitted. You watch their budding gifts with anxious vigilance; perhaps you rack your brain with thought, and your heart with care, to find the right work for them, and the means of setting them to it; and then a dread may seize you lest, after all, it should prove the wrong one, and their lives should go all astray. No doubt it is on the whole the gravest burden which God devolves on a man —the settlement of his children in life. It is sad enough to see a youth of promise chained down by stern necessity to dull and uncongenial tasks; and there is nothing gladder than to see a young spirit stirred by a high vocation to develope all its power. And when they see the wrecks with which the coasts of this life-sea are strewn, well may the parents tremble, and wrestle earnestly and importunately for the guidance and the help of God.

But parents may find some relief from the extreme pressure of the burden in the thought that—

I. The vital question concerns their children rather than their lot.

Get *them* out in the form of modest, earnest, industrious, courageous, kindly, godly lads and girls, and their lot, though not a question without care, may be trusted, in some measure, to settle itself as they grow to maturity. The main question concerns what they *are;* what they shall do is altogether a secondary matter in the scale. It is a far higher fulfilment of parental duty, and far more blessed in its fruits, to parent and to child, to get a sound, brave, high-minded boy or girl into a position which the world might reckon a humble one, but where they would have room and opportunity to fight their way on, than to get an idle, slovenly, luxurious cross-grained child into the vestibule of Dives, or on to the steps of a throne. Parents are altogether too anxious what they shall do with their children, and too little careful that they shall be what is true, good, and noble, whatever they do. The most consummate artists make by their manual cunning the commonest tools more effectual for working out their highest conceptions, than the finest prove in the hands of a dolt. Turner's etching needle, I have heard, was the prong of an old steel fork, stuck tightly into a common bit of wood. And so you may put a youth of a certain strain of nature and character where you will, he will handle his life-tools so as to command success. Therefore throw your strength *into* your children; send them forth inwardly furnished for life's battle, out of that armoury, the stores of which are dispensed by no niggard hand, and work will be found for them more easily than your anxious heart can believe. Faculty rarely waits for opportunity. Do *you* care for the faculty—physical, mental, and moral —and God in good time will show you its sphere.

Some of you may think that I spoke too absolutely in a former discourse, about laying up treasure for children, that they may inherit it when your work is done. But the conviction that, in the main, it does the devil's work, is forced upon me, I think, every year more clearly, by what I see of the miseries which hoarded treasures engender in families, and the sadly aimless, useless lives which they tempt men and women, not without native nobleness, to live. If it were possible to trace the history of great fortunes as they flow down from generation to generation, you would be filled with amazement at the strife and wretchedness which would be laid bare. The history of Spanish Philip's gold-glutted empire may point the moral. When the veil is lifted, and the secrets of the monarch's cabinet are exposed, you see one of the saddest spectacles which the sun shone upon in those days. The richest and most powerful prince in Christendom bemoaning his poverty and impotence, and thinking himself one of the most helpless and wretched mortals in the world.

At the same time, one sees plainly that it is not a question to be settled in a word. A wise provision for old age becomes an inheritance for the children; unless, indeed, the days should return, when men, having settled the young ones safe and warm in their new nests, felt that they might fairly take thought for the poor, the ignorant, the hungry, the shivering ones scattered about the world—the days in which men, having done their life-work nobly, and gathered an ample store, founded an hospital, a refuge, a college, a Magdalene's home, or a school for poor orphans, and left the blessing of such a legacy to their heirs. The thought may call forth a smile in these days. The splendid gifts which the men of old time delighted to offer to man and to God, are out of tune with our habits. The worse for us, I think; though there is grave danger—alas! there is danger everywhere—that such gifts may miss their mark. But the world is terribly full of ignorance, nakedness, deformity, starvation, and misery; our present methods fail to overtake the evil, and there must be some way surely in which a man, whose soul is moved of God to it, could devote his treasure wisely to the service of mankind. And if we could get children out into the world with natures in such sympathy with Christ's, that they would sum up a parent's good deeds with a joy which uncounted treasures could not kindle, and would hear the blessings of poor men on his name with a pride which the inheritance of a princedom could not stir, we should be far on towards the day which is dim enough in the distance still, when "*the Spirit shall be poured upon us from on high, and the wilderness be a fruitful field, and the fruitful field be counted for a forest. Then judgment shall dwell in the wilderness, and righteousness remain in the fruitful field. And the work of righteousness shall be peace; and the effect of righteousness, quietness and assurance for ever.*" I cannot see that the hoarding principle, the founding great families on great fortunes, is such a grand success, that it is foolish to ask if there be not some more excellent way. Nor can I see how on any other principle than this—the abasement of gold as a mere possession to the dirt from which it springs, and the exaltation of truth, righteousness, and love—the world is to grow into the likeness of a kingdom of heaven.

I know that when all is said and done by a Christian parent in earnest about his duty, grave and often crushing cares will still weigh upon his heart. Children *will* sometimes grow unkindly, and talent for any sort of work may be weak and poor. Words go but a little way to help any of us through the burden and the heat of life. But thus much I may say, with intense conviction, that the more a parent cares for what he lays up *in* the child, and the less he torments himself about what he can lay up *for* him, the richer will be the legacy which he will bequeath. Give all diligence to get the children out, nobly equipped for all good words and works, and then trust God to guide them into the nook of the vineyard in which He intends them to labour; for all such He has a prepared place. It is wonderful how the worst weight of the burden will be rolled away as you see strength and riches gathering within. Great peace will fall on your heart about their future, if your children are growing into a likeness which you can honour and delight in. Only look to the young shoots that they be clean and straight, with the sap pure and plentiful within, and then—

II. Plant them out where they will have air and light enough to grow.

Remember that you get them out distinctly that they may *grow*. Not that they may grow rich, famous, or powerful—that is as God wills; but that they may grow good, righteous, Christ-like—that is according to the will of God. The supreme question with a parent in sending a child forth, is growth and development—the growth of all that is worthy to grow, the destruction of all that is worthy to be destroyed. The "being" of the youth or maiden outweighs utterly the question of their getting, or the place which they can assume in society. What is mainly wanted is the eye clear—as the Saviour says, "single"—then there is sure to be light enough on the path. God is light, and in Him there is no darkness at all. His light is abroad everywhere; if we see it not, and things by it, it is because there is darkness within. If men get bewildered and worried about duty, you may be sure that there is some mist of pride, passion, or selfishness before the eye, which makes the outlines of things obscure. If a man has an idea that a fine position, the certainty of a rapid fortune, or a brilliant marriage, is a thing to be desired for its own sake, and to be weighed against the moral disadvantages which it may entail, the film has gathered before his sight, and there is no hope of his seeing the right path until it be cleared away.

The great work of the Saviour is this purging the inward eye from the humours of passion and selfishness; and it should be the earnest aim of all ministers of the gospel, not to say, "Do this or this, and it shall be well"—keeping men ever expectant of direction and in perpetual babyhood—but to clear the eye of these mists, that they may see what to do of themselves. The eye was given for seeing—to discern paths; but the devil has floated illusions before it, and paralysed the chief nerve of its power. The Lord tells us that we walk in a vain show; we take shadows for substances, idle imaginations for things. He seeks to restore the lost power of vision, that we may see Jesus, and follow Him in the way.

Follow Him in caring supremely for the souls' health of your children, wherever you may send them forth. No matter about the struggle, the uphill fight, if that which is born of God in them gets air and sunlight, breathes itself in healthy exercise, and suns itself in the glow of the love of God. By these things men live; these make the inner blessedness which smiles on through sorrows, and the want of these makes the inner cursedness which moans in purple, and gnaws the heart-strings even in the courts of kings. Take true measure of this. What is it which makes the blessing in life, what makes the curse? Look the reality in the face—search your own conscience—search the records of lives that are open to you—search them fearlessly, and say, is there one who has made position or wealth his idol, for whose life—and I care not how high fortune may have lifted him—you would exchange your own? Have you a shadow of doubt as to what lies at the bottom of nine-tenths of the misery of the world, of its loveless homes, its broken hearts, its reckless lives, its dull satiety, its hateful selfishness—what but this occursed grasping at gold? Fathers and mothers, who have children to get out into life, shut yourselves up to this question, answer it to your own souls as solemnly as you would answer it at the great day of judgment, and shudder back from the thought of sacrificing that dear heart, all unprophetic of its future, to the demon who is preying on the immortal life of mankind.

There are mothers, with a bright troop of girls around them, whose crowning triumph apparently is, to "get them off their hands." Perhaps they may find it easier to get them off their hands than off their hearts. A clever mother, who gives her mind to it, can manage the first well enough; she can angle for a good *parti*, and secure him with dexterous, infallible art. What he *is*, if he be decently presentable, is nothing; what he can do to make a woman's life what it was meant to be, is nothing. Has he a position? Is it a good match? "Then he must be secured at any hazard, and there will be another of my girls off my hands." The basest traffic which is carried on upon earth is carried on here in England. It is baser here than elsewhere, for women in England know better what womanhood means. But it is easier, as I have said, to get a daughter off the hands than off the heart. I have seen girls, whom I had known in the happy springtime of their lives, after a year or two of brilliant marriage, so worn, so wan, so unspeakably woeful and hopeless, that their look has quite haunted me. Beware, mothers, beware of the pallid, wrecked, writhing faces which may peer through the gloom when it gathers around your death-bed: happy if you can leave them there; happy if you can get them off your hearts through eternity.

A good position! a good business! a good match! O my friends! we must learn from God what is good; we must take His counsel into our hearts—that counsel which all the experience in the universe affirms, and must affirm eternally—before we can see our way. But once believe in the good, "the better part," the blessed part, "which shall never be taken away"—only admit *that* into the inner sanctuary of the heart—it is like the unfurling of a mist from a sunlit landscape—the ways are there clear and straight from your very feet.

Do not mistake the true scope of my words. In speaking of grasping, of hoarding, I am not speaking of getting. If men are to enter business, they must set before themselves a fair hope of gain. I do not know what is to take a man down to the mill-wheel daily, but some clear prospect of success in buying and selling and getting gain. If a man works hard, it will be for "returns;" and if there be energy and capacity, the returns will roll freely in with their freight of profit. He is bound to take it with a thankful heart, and to use it as God's gift for elevating and enlarging the range of his life. Nothing is a greater mistake than to suppose that every implied or expressed command in the Bible, is addressed as a literal direction to every member of the human race. Every man is no more bound to "sell all that he hath and give to the poor," than he is bound to be an apostle. Let every man be as his gift is; according to the Scripture precept, "*Let every man, wherein he is called, therein abide with God.*" But spend the fruits of your labour with a liberal hand. Spend them on whatever enlarges faculty, enriches life, and mitigates the sorrows of the poor. Make your home larger, more cheerful, more graceful, more free to a wide circle of friends, with the gold that flows in upon you. Keep it flowing, and all will go well; circulation is the principle of life. But don't hoard it for the children, who, when their eyes are open, as they will be one day, will curse it, and will remember with bitterness that the only elevation which you cared to seek for them was one whose base platform was gold.

One main condition of success in the getting children out into life—the true success, winning a fair position for living what heaven calls life—is the earnestness which you may kindle within them, by making them in a measure the sharers of your confidence, and opening to them the secret chambers of your own heart. I think that one chief element of the parental art is timely and judicious confidence. The best preparation for the burden and the struggle into which getting out into life will usher them, is the knowledge in some wise measure of what it costs the elders to live—costs, I mean in the highest sense, effort, patience, and hope. But even about the lower things of life, the confidence is not wasted. Boys and girls are content to know that their parents manage to live somehow, that somehow money seems to come when it is wanted, and that things go on upon the whole in a very natural and comfortable way. And how should they think otherwise, unless the veil is a little lifted? Their daily bread, their daily pleasures, come to them much as the sunlight comes; they know nothing of the dust and the sweat of the battle that wins them; just as we think little of the burden which presses on the Hand that daily rolls round the spheres.

It is well that as the intelligence unfolds, the young people should know something of what the order and comfort of the home is costing—something of what the father and mother talk over, with broken voices and clasped hands sometimes, when the children have left them and the cares of the day are done—that they may not think that life is quite a holiday pastime, and may see that the noblest thing a man has to do in this world is to toil patiently and suffer bravely, that others may be housed, clothed, fed, and trained for God.

But much wisdom is needed here. Few things are more purely cruel than to kill young hope and joy. We may easily make children anxious, sorrowful, and probably distrustful, in their spring, by weighing them too early with the burden of our cares. A wise parent will keep the veil of the inner sanctuary drawn, lest their young, gay footsteps enter, and they get a shock which may cripple them for life; but he is bound, too, to lift it partially, in wise measures, that life's richer meanings may lie open to them, and that they may not be caught at a disadvantage, or be disheartened when they discover for themselves how much wise and righteous living may cost. Communion of spirit between parent and child is the best training for life. Treat them like children when they are yearning for the bread of your confidence, and when they feel the stirring within them of manly and womanly powers, and you drive them to other and less helpful comrades. Are there any veils thicker than those which parents constantly suffer to fall, between their own inner nature and the inner nature of their children? Why is it that children so frequently find it easier to open their hearts to strangers, than to those who are set in their homes to be to them in the place of God? Make them your comrades as Christ made His disciples, opening to them your heart of hearts as their nature unfolds; while at the same time you share their sports and pastimes, and keep your interest keen in all their pursuits and pleasures; taking as much of your own boyhood or girlhood as you can on with you through life.

Very precious, too, may be the ministry of a sister to a brother just at the time when he is getting out into the world; when his knowledge of the world is beginning to widen, and he first feels the pressure of those temptations from which girls at home are mercifully shielded, and which are making such havoc of the moral and physical power of our people. If the girls in our homes would betake themselves more freely to the fountain of which we have spoken, and would breathe the atmosphere of a pure, noble, and gracious womanhood around them, the harlotries of the world would but disgust where they now allure and destroy. It seems to me sadly neglected in homes, this power of brother and sister to help each other, to bear each other up in their highest endeavours and aspirations, and be the complement of each other's life. It ought to be the purest and most beautiful of relations; there is no burden in it, it is all help and joy. It is the best likeness which we have on earth to the relations of the heavenly world, where "*they neither marry nor are given in marriage, but are as the angels of God.*" All pure love in its first virgin blush takes the hue of this relationship. The young lovers are sister and brother in the earliest and perhaps the happiest days of their fellowship; and it would be hard to over-estimate the power of a pure and high-minded sister to guard her brother, by the reverence which her purity inspires, from some of his most besetting temptations. As far as my observation has reached, it appears to me that the purest and truest-hearted men that I have known, have been those whose sisters have set before them the highest image of a woman in their own homes. And thus I come back to the old principle—Women, be yourselves, and rule the world!

Young friends, boys and girls, blooming into young men and women, be content " to hasten slowly," as the old Greek proverb has it. One of the most precious beliefs which a youth or maiden can take with them into the arena, is a belief in the virtue of patience, in the need of repression, in the wisdom of deepening the hold of the root fibres, before the head lifts itself bravely in the sun. One of the hardest words, naturally enough, for the eager young spirit to believe in is, "Wait." There is the gleaming many-tinted iris, spanning the unknown faëry world which the child dreams of as life. A rosy light floods all the air. Eden was not a fairer bower to the first human children, than is the world to each of its young dreamers. They look on this fair earth and this wonderful life, as Israel on the land of golden promise; they have had vision of it too from the Pisgah summit of a child's day dreams. "The Paradise is there, let me enter it swiftly;

father, mother, it is mine, it will not escape me if I seize it now." There is a pining eagerness in a youth of promise to cut a swift path to these glorious gardens, whose golden apples a hundred generations have missed. What matter millenniums of futile effort, wretched failure, broken hope? What matter! Each young spirit starts with unabated ardour and freshness on the quest. He is sure that life will yield to him the secret which all have missed. "The land of promise is there beyond the river. Courage! its cities and treasures will soon be in our hands."

And there is no girl's paradise without an Adam, nor boy's without an Eve. "Every soul," says Emerson, "is a celestial Venus to every other soul." But boys and girls believe in the elective affinities; in the sister soul, the twin, whom it is the aim and the bliss of life to meet. Well, I believe in it, too. But it is rarely that the twin souls stumble on each other at once. There is a halo round all things to the boy's burning vision, and the first fair form or fair soul—for boys and girls care more about souls than forms—which strikes the fancy, shines with a peerless splendour. "The problem of life is solved!" they cry; "with this Adam, this Eve, the wilderness will be as the garden of the Lord."

And the parents' word is "Wait;" at which youth rebels. The cherubim and the flaming sword not seldom appear through the mandate of a hard necessity, or a parent's stern behests. Now, I am not so foolish as to volunteer much advice to hearts in such a case. Indeed, I have not much faith in rules, directions, or counsels of any sort, least of all about these high matters, except such as tell on the being, and fit it to clear its own path, and to see its own way. I believe, on the whole, firmly in early marriages and an uphill fight. But I believe, above all, in waiting —waiting that costs resolution and endeavour, and it may be sharp pain, that souls may be sure of themselves and of each other before they mate. Love, like all other noble things, gains immensely by endurance, by submission. Those whose wise experience is holding you back, in tender care, from a too eager scaling of the gate of Paradise, are rendering your love a noble service, if it be rooted deeply in the soul's elections; and are sparing you the sorrow of sorrows, if, as may well happen, and as a little patience may prove, it be not. Do not be too ready to believe that life's great problem is solved in a moment; and do not grudge effort and patience, heroic it may be—and the unknown heroisms are of highest account in the eye of Heaven—to be assured that the problem is solved rightly, and solved for ever. The twin souls are one through eternity. But how many of them on earth are one?

With equal earnestness would I urge on young men going forth into life the need of patience, that they may lay the foundation of a manly independence, by toiling long and thoroughly at the mere drudgery of their calling, before they think themselves fit for the higher forms. The *ignis fatuus* of clever young men is a spurious and baseless independence, tempting them to play the master before they have learned the lessons of service thoroughly, and to handle results before they have made the secrets of the processes their own. Impatience of apprenticeship, using the word in a wide sense, is what distinguishes these eager and insubordinate times from the great days of old. There are few who rule nobly, partly because there are few who care to serve long. You have to be builders of a temple of life. "Edify yourselves," "edify one another," is a favourite exhortation of Scripture about life. A builder grudges no toil that he spends on the foundations. Edify your temple firmly from the first. Take the wisdom of the elders as your guide, long after you have felt the first strong temptation to think yourself the wiser. Refuse not the yoke, long after you have thought that you could play the master bravely yourself. Build for a long future. Life may be short here, but it is long there. None lay the foundations broad and deep enough; none believe more than feebly and vaguely in eternity. The masters there, I think, will be chosen from the band who were not afraid of a life-long service here. "Friend, go up higher," will not be the greeting of the boys and girls who thought themselves fit at the first start for the highest rooms.

For understand, lastly and solemnly, that you are getting out into a life whose range is as wide as the universe and as long as eternity. Understand farther, that until you have let the solemn eternal light shine in upon it, you cannot comprehend aright the most trivial tasks and the most common cares. Nothing with which man has to do can take its true size and form, unless it be projected upon the horizon of eternity. You step out into the great eternal universe, when you step out of the fold which sheltered your childhood. Your every thought, your every work, thenceforth has issues which range on with your being while that being endures. Speak merrily to your soul, if you will, and say, " Soul, thou hast much goods laid up for many years; take thy fill, eat, drink, and be merry." But remember the morning after the summons, " This night thy soul shall be required of thee;" remember the inevitable morning, and the day or the night—the day of bliss or the night of weeping—that will never end. There are wonders and splendours, such as an angel may hardly prevail to look upon, within the field of your future, as you tramp through the round of your common tasks—tempted to think, perhaps, that a dog's life has more interest and variety than yours. Make it a dog's life, and they vanish from the field of your vision for ever. Make it a man's life, and pay the cost for a little space—" endure hardness, as a good soldier of Jesus Christ"—and one day you will range with exulting triumphant power through all the pathways of the new creation, and search out the glory which is wisely veiled from mortal sight, whose unveiling will be the apocalypse of eternity. Get out into life with the solemn, ennobling sense that you are getting out into life eternal, and weigh every pleasure and pain of this world in the balances whose measures are square with the standards of God.

IX.

THE FAMILY MINISTRY.

"When the ear heard me, then it blessed me; and when the eye saw me, it gave witness to me; because I delivered the poor that cried, and the fatherless, and him that had none to help him. The blessing of him that was ready to perish came upon me: and I caused the widow's heart to sing for joy. I put on righteousness, and it clothed me: my judgment was as a robe and a diadem. I was eyes to the blind, and feet was I to the lame. I was a father to the poor, and the cause which I knew not I searched out."—JOB xxix. 11-16.

"FREELY *ye have received, freely give,*" is the Christian law. Blessed with a dear home life yourselves, purify and gladden poor homes around. The great hope for society is, that the influence of a pure and noble home life may descend, and flow through all the squalid, wretched households, which are the fruitful mothers of crime and sorrow. A Christian household ill comprehends its vocation, if it is not training the boys and girls which grow up in it, to be wise as well as diligent and devoted ministers to the poor. The nature and method of this ministry will be the topic of the present discourse.

It is nobly sketched in the words which I have taken for my text. The chapter contains probably the finest picture of the life of an eastern patriarch, which has ever been painted by the hand of man. The whole book of Job, in fact, lets us into the secret of an age and a mode of life which is about the polar opposite of our own. The patriarchal age is but lightly touched in the historical books of Scripture. Or rather, I should say, what is said about it has a distinct reference to a Divine purpose which, running through it, hastened on to a goal beyond. The book of Genesis is but the exordium of the book of the legal dispensation, which itself is but the vestibule of the dispensation of the gospel. It contains notices of the life and manners of the patriarchal age which are of the highest value, as it traces the fortunes of the elect race, to which was confided the leading part in the drama of the history of the world. But in the book of Job we have notices which are more valuable still. Here the author dwells fondly on the patriarchal age for its own sake, and lingers over its manners and simple incidents with a tender and loving hand. Job and the race to which he belonged are out of the line of the elect people. They have but a remote kindred with them, and their life and that of their whole race could be but at the best an episode in history. There is no pressing forward to a purpose here. The details are touched with the skill and care of an artist who has time and room to present a complete portrait; and the result is a picture of the manners, the thoughts, the life, of an old patriarchal chieftain in his tribe, which is unique in history.

It seems to have been painted by a man who was familiar with a state of society which somewhat sadly contrasted with it. As Tacitus, in the corrupt society of the Empire, lingers fondly over the pure and simple morals of the German tribes, so the writer of this book, full of the cares and burdens of a national statesman, and observant of the vices and miseries of national life, dwells on this image of a grand old Edomite patriarch, as a witness and a warning to his times. If the writer was Moses—I am not ignorant of the difficulties attaching to the supposition, but they seem to me far from decisive—we can understand it perfectly. To a man steeped in all the learning of the Egyptians, and sated with their splendid and luxurious civilisation, it would be like a breath of pure, fresh mountain air, to come across the record of such a life. What a grand picture of the Bedouin chief, the father of his tribe, is presented here: "*Moreover, Job continued his parable, and said, Oh that I were as in months past, as in the days when God preserved me; when His candle shined upon my head, and when by His light I walked through darkness; as I was in the days of my youth, when the secret of God was upon my tabernacle; when the Almighty was yet with me, when my children were about me; when I washed my steps with butter, and the rock poured me out rivers of oil; when I went out to the gate through the city, when I prepared my seat in the street! The young men saw me, and hid themselves; and the aged arose, and stood up. The princes refrained talking, and laid their hand on their mouth. The nobles held their peace, and their tongue cleaved to the roof of their mouth. When the ear heard me, then it blessed me; and when the eye saw me, it gave witness to me; because I delivered the poor that cried, and the fatherless, and him that had none to help him.*

11*

The blessing of him that was ready to perish came upon me: and I caused the widow's heart to sing for joy. I put on righteousness, and it clothed me: my judgment was as a robe and a diadem. I was eyes to the blind, and feet was I to the lame. I was a father to the poor; and the cause which I knew not I searched out. And I brake the jaws of the wicked, and plucked the spoil out of his teeth. Then I said, I shall die in my nest, and I shall multiply my days as the sand. My root was spread out by the waters, and the dew lay all night upon my branch. My glory was fresh in me, and my bow was renewed in my hands. Unto me men gave ear, and waited, and kept silence at my counsel. After my words they spake not again; and my speech dropped upon them. And they waited for me as for the rain; and they opened their mouth wide as for the latter rain. If I laughed on them, they believed it not; and the light of my countenance they cast not down. I chose out their way and sat chief, and dwelt as a king in the army, as one that comforteth the mourners" (Job xxix. 1–25).

This picture belongs to a time when government was—as all government was once—paternal. Much which it is hard to characterise as other than pure nonsense, has been written about the social contract, and probably by the sentimental infidels whose works prepared the way for the first French Revolution. The original social contract, even the idea of a compact—except such as grows out of pre-existing relations, as was the case with the pilgrim fathers—is a mere fiction. The fontal type of all government, the mould in which it was originally cast, is the rule of a father in his home. Men soon outgrow this. Society gets too wide, and too wise. It becomes too capable of self-government for one man to rule it father-like; no man can sustain this relation to a wide and cultivated community of his fellow-men. The effort becomes the parent of the most absolute and soul-debasing tyranny, as may be seen at this moment in France. Society, conscious that it has outgrown the paternal rule, has all sorts of devices to get itself tolerably governed; but they all blunder utterly in the way, and miss utterly of the end, if they fail to discern that the fundamental idea of government is the father's rule; and that the kind of order which needs to be established in human society is the loving order which a father maintains in a home.

Now, no government, as government must be

in a complicated and highly civilised community like ours, can fulfil this function—can take this fatherly oversight of men. A chieftain of a tribe may do it; a ruler of a great nation cannot. And one would watch very sadly the growth of a community to a magnitude which precludes the exercise of the paternal function by the government, and makes the freest independence of the individual members, even the basest and most foolish, the test of the development of the people, but for the belief that a Wiser and Stronger than any human father is ruling; and that He is employing the various organs of the national life to make His fatherly will the governing principle in the conduct of its public affairs. If, as man drops the sceptre and confesses that the task of rule is too hard, we cannot believe that a higher Hand is grasping it, dark indeed would be our vision of the aspect and prospect of the world.

And that God may rule in states, that the moral element of the problem may not be lost sight of, that the Fatherly care and influence may not quite vanish from the wider sphere of the national life, God has founded an institution, in which spiritual elements and interests are predominant; which takes His Word as its statute-book of commandment, and seeks to be filled with His Spirit as the principle of its life. As the secular sphere developes itself according to the instincts and visible interests of men, the Church is ordained to keep God's truth before it, and to bring the benign influence of the Father and the Redeemer of spirits to bear on the order and progress of society. The Church is not other than the world in God's ultimate thought and purpose. But so long as the world seeks worldly inspiration in all its activities and achievements, God purposes that there shall be those in it who shall bear witness for higher truths, and bring higher influences to bear on men. The end will be reached, and the two spheres will blend in one, when "*None shall hurt and none shall destroy in all God's holy mountain; but the earth shall be full of the knowledge of the Lord, as the waters cover the sea.*"

By the Church, I mean simply, the body of believers who yield themselves to be the organs of God's Spirit in the world, whose desire and aim is to make His influence, as the Father and Redeemer, the ruling power in society. The Church can bring this Fatherly element into the ordering and government of mankind, because it is, what no mere ruler or magistrate can be, God's instrument, His organ, rather, for the spiritual rule and guidance of men. The Christian element in society—the fontal fire of which is kept pure and bright on the hearth of the Christian household—seeks to supply the want, of which, as society enlarges its borders, grows wider, wiser, and more complex, it becomes painfully conscious —the want of a Father's rule. Job was priest and king in his tribe; Abraham was priest and king in his family—the germ of a tribe; but no man or men can be, even in the measure which was possible for them, priest and king to a nation or to the world. The one Priest and King of humanity is Christ; and His organ, His body, is the Church, which is destined one day to transform the world, and then to be lost in it. The earthly fountains of its vital power are Christian homes. They are the eyes and the hands of the Church; they feed its strength, and they conduct it; they are the organs of its ministry, the channels of its life.

Training for ministry to the world should be one main feature of the higher culture of Christian households. To study and fulfil this patriarchal function is one great purpose of their existence. I confine myself in this connexion to the consideration of the ministry to the poor, which is so graphically set forth in the text; for it is in connexion with the poor that the most difficult problems of society arise. How thoroughly it is recognised as the chief work of the Divine Ruler, to right the wrongs and relieve the miseries of the poor, a thousand passages of the Scripture declare as emphatically as this: "*He shall have dominion also from sea to sea, and from the river unto the ends of the earth. They that dwell in the wilderness shall bow before Him; and His enemies shall lick the dust. The kings of Tarshish and of the isles shall bring presents: the kings of Sheba and Seba shall offer gifts. Yea, all kings shall fall down before him; all nations shall serve Him. For He shall deliver the needy when he crieth; the poor also, and him that hath no helper. He shall spare the poor and needy, and shall save the souls of the needy. He shall redeem their soul from deceit and violence; and precious shall their blood be in His sight*" (Ps. lxxii. 8–14).

I purpose to offer some practical remarks on the passage prefixed to this discourse, to stimulate and guide this ministry of the Christian household

—the microcosm of which the Church is the macrocosm—as much as is in my power.

I. The duty of the Church, the Christian element of society, to search out the cause of the poor, and to be a father to them.

I dwell specially on the searching it out. The energy and the self-denial, the patience and the power of endurance, which the searching out the cause or the case of the poor demands, can be supplied in constant measure but from one spring. I imagine that if we could have set before the eye of the mind at any moment, as vividly as if it were before the natural eye, the miseries, the torments, the agony of body, mind, and spirit, which millions of our fellow-creatures are enduring through poverty and what springs from it, we should rush to the rescue with mad haste, lest God should inquire for all these groans, these tears, this blood, at our hands. No sleep for us to-night, till some naked ones had been clothed, some starving ones had been fed, some shivering ones had been cherished before a cheery fire, and a taste at least had been given to some poor outcast of all that God, in His infinite goodness to us, has granted us in our home. But, not seeing it, we realize it but dimly. We know well enough that there is such a thing as the misery of the poor in the background, just as we know that there is Death. We never search for him, but we feel sometimes his chill breath, and see his awful shadow flung over the glowing landscape of our lives. And so this dread shadow of poverty crosses us sometimes, but we hasten out of its gloom into the warm sunlight once more. It is one of the things which we are prone to put by in the dark corner, and look at as little as we may. But now let us hear God's word: "*If thou forbear to deliver them that are drawn unto death, and those that are ready to be slain; if thou sayest, Behold, we knew it not; doth not He that pondereth the heart consider it? and He that keepeth thy soul, doth not He know it? and shall not He render to every man according to his works*" (Prov. xxiv. 11, 12)

It is our business, our plainest duty, to search it out. The world does not know, and half of it does not care. But we are bound to know. The home is a field of the noblest culture, and it is the organ of the divinest ministry. Let it neglect the last, and by the sternest of all laws, the first is lost. The home is constantly called the nursery of the Church. It is something more. The old Jewish synagogue was constituted by families. So in a very high sense were the old Puritan churches. The home is the church, not in miniature but in microcosm; that is, it is a complete Church within its sphere. And through the home and its Christian charities the ministry of the Church must be mainly accomplished. And here is its first office, to search out the cause of the poor. We are bound to know it, and to let the world know it. We are bound to bring the dark facts out of their darkness, and set them before the world in the full light of day. One of the first duties of a Christian household is to resolve to know for itself, and to make others know, the state of its poor around. I say its poor. "*The poor ye have always with you.*" They are Christ's charge to those whom He has enriched and blessed. Its poor are those within sound of its voice, within touch of its hand. The only, the all-sufficient plea is poverty and wretchedness; our sect, our dependents, our neighbours!—Christ knows nothing of such limitations. He tells us only of "the poor." Even the Jew, narrow and exclusive as his disposition is popularly, but most falsely, held to have been, did not dare to limit his responsibility to the poor even of his own nation. "*And when ye reap the harvest of your land, thou shalt not wholly reap the corners of thy field, neither shalt thou gather the gleanings of thy harvest. And thou shalt not glean thy vineyard, neither shalt thou gather every grape of thy vineyard; thou shalt leave them for the poor and stranger; I am the Lord your God. . . . . And if a stranger sojourn with thee in your land, ye shall not vex him. But the stranger that dwelleth with you, shall be unto you as one born among you, and thou shalt love him as thyself; for ye were strangers in the land of Egypt. I am the Lord your God*" (Lev. xix. 9, 10, 33, 34). "*At the end of three years thou shalt bring forth all the tithe of thine increase the same year, and shalt lay it up within thy gates, and the Levite (because he hath no part nor inheritance with thee), and the stranger, and the fatherless, and the widow, which are within thy gates, shall come, and shall eat, and be satisfied; that the Lord thy God may bless thee in all the work of thine hand which thou doest*" (Deut. xiv. 28, 29). God taught him the secret of a large-hearted charity; and shall we be more narrow and selfish than the Jew? God forbid. "*For we know the grace of our Lord Jesus, how that though He was rich, yet for our sakes He* became poor, that we through His poverty might be rich."

But we live in a strangely complicated state of society. It is said that one half of the world does not know how the other half lives. It is a liberal estimate. How many neither know nor care? It was otherwise of old. Job knew every poor one, every vicious one, in his tribe; he knew how to deal with them, and he knew further that the responsibility of their condition rested in some serious measure at his door. The old patriarchal feeling survived in a Roman bishop as late as the end of the sixth century. A man died, starved to death, in the streets of Rome, and Gregory the Great, the Roman bishop, imposed on himself the heaviest penances, and interdicted himself from the discharge of the sacred offices, because it had been possible that such a thing should happen even in the vast city in which he was Father, Papa, Pope.

In the middle ages something of this close oversight was possible. Rich and poor lived much together in the same quarters, in the same streets. In our county towns you will still see, where railroad life has not effaced the last traces of the past, the noble mansion, the town-house of the great county family, with a hovel leaning against its side. In truth towns grew originally, through the clustering of the poor for work and shelter near the great man's castle gate. And you will constantly see still a row of poor cottages, then a handsome house or two, and then a row of poor cottages again. The rich and the poor lived near each other, and there was a fair chance at any rate of a rich man's knowing the poor man's needs. But our luxurious living has changed all that. We have our rich quarters and our poor quarters, with few ministering footsteps passing between. We have our squares of splendid palaces, without the disfigurement of one poor man's dwelling; we have wide tracts of penury, vice, and wretchedness, without the ornament of one rich man's home. The rich draw together, and the poor are driven together; and a great gulf has been opened between them, which benign ministries have begun to fill.

But our Tyburnias and Belgravias, whose dreary monotony is some penalty on their splendour, involve inevitably our Rookeries and Ragfairs. Every great "quarter" built for riches, means that poverty, want, withering toil and bitter sorrow, have extended their area too. The natural tendencies of the age are to the separation of the classes. The Christian office is to wed them again, to reintroduce them to each other, and to make them feel in more loving ways than God's judgments—such as cholera, typhus, smallpox, and the like—employ, that they belong to each other, and that at the bottom their interests are one.

And the first step to this is to seek them out; to discover poverty and misery in their lairs, and bring them out before the face of the world, into the light of day. Every Christian household ought to have its little band of searchers, and ought to make known in quiet ways, as opportunity offers, the estate of the poor. The truth is, it only needs to be known to be mended. The searching out is the chief matter. The City Missions and kindred agencies have searched out the condition of the masses of our city poor so effectually, and made known so widely the knowledge they have gained, that there is a new stir through the whole sphere of society, and a thousand hands are now stretched forth in every direction to seek and to save. And Christ is the moving spirit of it all, though many name not the name of Christ while they are busy in the work.

But Christianity has done thus much for Christian society; the words, "*Am I my brother's keeper?*" can never again be uttered as a bar to the ministry of society to its poor. The world now could not live on and go about its tasks, were it set sternly face to face with their actual condition. The evil once known in all its dark dimensions, some help must be found, some cure.

Be it yours to know, that you may tell. Don't be satisfied with the vague knowledge with which multitudes of professed philanthropists content themselves. See it for yourselves, women of Christian households, while the men are about their daily tasks; see it for yourselves and touch it, and if is a bitter sight, don't turn away. Let the bitterness sink into your heart. It was a bitter sight to Christ, but He did not turn from it; He became its fellow; He bore all the bitterness of it life-long, and now He sends you, His ministers, to help Him by Christian charity to bear all its bitterness away. Study the problem closely; acquaint yourself, as among your first and most sacred Christian duties, with the cause of your poor.

II. See that you bear a hand to help it.

I find the deepest suggestion on this point from the narrative in Mark: "*And straightway the father of the child cried out, and said with tears, Lord, I believe; help Thou mine unbelief. When Jesus saw that the people came running together, He rebuked the foul spirit, saying unto him, Thou dumb and deaf spirit, I charge thee, come out of him, and enter no more into him. And the spirit cried, and rent him sore, and came out of him: and he was as one dead; insomuch that many said, He is dead. But Jesus took him by the hand, and lifted him up; and he arose*" (Mark ix. 24–27).

Hand help! That is what the poor want; that is what the Lord calls for; that is what the Church must afford, if she is to give free play and healthy exercise to her noblest powers. Understand what I mean. Giving is the smallest and easiest part of Christian charity. Time is far more precious, and effort is far more precious, than money, to hard-worked men. And money may be given lavishly to save time and trouble, and may very easily be, nay, it too constantly is, a curse instead of a blessing to the poor. The Lord had no money to give, nor would He make any. This last is among the most significant features of His ministry. And the poorest Christian ministers are probably those who, at this moment, are doing the most for the help of the poor. The poor are commonly their own worst enemies. Their own improvidence, carelessness, and vice, share fully with the condition of society the responsibility of their state. They are very far from being their true friends who are afraid to tell them so—who will throw a sop of charity to meet their momentary need, and to win their passing gratitude, instead of tenderly but firmly pressing on them the recognition of the evil habits and passions, out of which, after all, nine-tenths of their miseries spring. To cure an evil habit, to brighten a sullen temper, to conquer a vicious propensity, in the poor subjects of your ministry, is to give something which is infinitely more precious than gold; it is a gift which they may bear on with them into eternity.

And to do this you must be, like Job, a friend to them. You must hear the narrative of their circumstances, you must observe carefully their habits, and you must speak, as only a friend can speak, home to their consciences and their hearts. That is putting a hand to the work. Some put only a face to it. They enter, with an expression of lofty condescension, the poor man's garret, and look infinite superiority while they lecture him on his follies and sins. I am persuaded that very much of the bitterness, with which intelligent and independent working men speak of those whom they call "the saints," is due to the quiet insolence with which pious visitors, often with the best intentions, intrude their presence and advice at unseemly seasons in humble homes. Those who will take poverty by the hand must take the burden of it upon them, and will be made solemn and sad as they feel its weight. Nor must it be made altogether the work of the women, though they will be the chief almoners of the Church and of heaven. Time may be scarce and costly with the prosperous man of business. "I must stick to my business," he will be likely to say, "or my means of sending help in any form will fail." By all means. This ought he to do, but not to leave the other undone. The use of a little portion of his time in searching out the cause of the poor, will pay him infinitely better than any business use which he may make of it. If you want to hallow your business, don't slave at it, and don't let it make a slave of you. Leave it, and the gain it might bring, some hour or two, at any rate, in the week; and go, see for yourselves how poor men and women are living, how they are compelled to live by the very conditions which make it possible that colossal commercial fortunes may be amassed. See for yourselves how women will fight to get near a door where slop-work is given out, which will yield them some sixpence a-day by worse than a slave's toil. Do not be content to hear; go and see, and put forth a hand to help them to a better work. At any rate, if you cannot do much in the way of helping, bear the pain of seeing it and touching it, and let others share the pain. When society fairly takes up the burden, and feels its weight, something effectual will be done.

And the real, the radical mischief, is one which the children of Christian homes, beyond all others, may help to cure. It is the wretched home life which is the chief parent of the drunkenness, the recklessness, the wastefulness, the apathy, which make such havoc of the means and the happiness of multitudes of our labouring poor. The dirt, the closeness, the damp, and the darkness, of the dens which hundreds of thousands in our great cities are forced to couch in and to occupy as homes, drive the men forth to dissipation, and break down the women's courage and strength. Clean, sweet, airy, cheerful habitations, must be the foundation of all vital improvement. And the housewifely maiden, trained in wise thrift and management, who shall help a poor woman to keep some cleanly order in her close lodging, in spite of the well-nigh overwhelming pressure of her lot—who shall teach her some thrifty ways, give a new idea of the management of the children, and see that she has a clean corner by a bright hearth-fire for the husband when he comes home from his tasks—is rendering society, as well as her poor sister, a noble service, and is helping effectually towards the solution of the most perplexed problem of our times. I never shall forget the emphasis with which a husband whose wife had been taken in hand by a wise, kind woman after the fashion I have described, and who had been thus weaned from the gin-shop, once exclaimed to me, " I never knew what it was to have a home before."

Reform the homes, and the poor will reform themselves, and society will be renewed at the spring. Every fresh hand put forth to the work, every fresh helper who will give personal ministry, brings us nearer to the time when the bitterness of poverty will cease out of the land; when society in the name of Christ, and by the Spirit of Christ, shall rise up and put it away for ever. It can be done; it will be done one day. If every master, every capitalist, every employer of labour were a Christ-like man, and every workman industrious and upright, where were the miseries of the poor? The root of them all is not in things, but in souls.

III. Believe that the blessing of the poor and of him that is ready to perish, is the noblest record which can appear for you on high. "*Then said He also to him that bade Him, When thou makest a dinner or a supper, call not thy friends, or thy brethren, neither thy kinsmen, nor thy rich neighbours; lest they also bid thee again, and a recompense be made thee. But when thou makest a feast, call the poor, the maimed, the lame, the blind: and thou shalt be blessed; for they cannot recompense thee: for thou shalt be recompensed at the resurrection of the just* (Luke xiv. 12–14).

We have come to believe that such words are hyperbole. That they simply mean in general that a blessing will attend on charity. But as for any special recompense for special acts, which the text seems to promise, it is against the genius of Christianity, and attributes an unworthy minuteness of reckoning to God. One might think so, if one did not see how close the cause of the poor is to the heart of the Great Father. If it be to Christ's brethren that you offer this ministry, if it be a clearing up of much that is awfully dark and doubtful about the ways of God, we can comprehend the sentence as it stands. Call these poor ones together and entertain them, you are entertaining them for the Lord; that is what He would do, along with deeper things, to give them a moment's honest gladness. He does it through you, He confesses Himself your debtor, and He is not one to forget that debt in the great day of eternity. I use very strong and absolute language here. I cannot help it. It is not I, but Scripture: "*He that hath pity on the poor lendeth to the Lord, and that which he hath given will He pay him again.*"

It is there, plain as words can make it. Man *may* make God his debtor, and in but one way. And if the case of the poor be a great sorrow to the Father's heart, a great difficulty in the way of His government, and a great burden to heavenly spirits, one can understand how it should be so. He who helps God with the poor helps indeed. Be not afraid to invest largely in those bonds; heaven seals them in its own chancery, and principal and interest will be richly repaid. Of all the words that can be spoken in the heavenly assembly about a man or a community, there are none that can compare with these, "He is a poor man's friend." "*He hath dispersed abroad, he hath given to the poor, his righteousness endureth for ever.*" About what other works that a man's hand can do, is such a sentence written in the word of God?

I know that I may be thought to be speaking injudiciously here, as though a foundation might be laid in good works for acceptance with God. But the Spirit saw what use could be made of these words when He moved His servant to write them, and He did not withhold his hand. Are we so much wiser than He? I am little afraid, to tell the truth, of much mischief on this side. If men will put their hands to the work, will take the burden of it on their own hearts, it will empty them of self-conceit and self-righteousness, or nothing will. No, the danger is not in this direction. The danger is, lest in these days men should despise these unseen rewards, these invisible wreaths of honour, smiling at them in their hearts as dreams or superstitious fancies, things meet enough to be pursued by saints and women, but mere follies to busy, acute, and practical men. Thus we men are prone to think of the account which it is said heaven keeps with the friends of the poor!

I believe, however, in most substantial repayments here. None have ever been beggared by their charities, and none have ever been left helpless in their needs who were known as poor men's friends. It is the very richest inheritance which a man can lay up for his children, the reputation of a liberal soul. "*The liberal soul shall be made fat, and by liberal things he shall stand.*" I believe that, in its secret soul, the world holds those in highest honour who have most helped its poor. If ever they need, it delights to repay the debt. The surest of all banks is this—the blessing of poor men. God keeps the deposits. There is no measure of the interest of that exchequer; for ten talents nobly used, ten cities. And remember the day will come when the last cheque has been signed, when the last bill has been drawn, when the last coin has been fingered. Gold has become but dirt to you, it will glitter for you no more for ever. "£100,000 for another month of life, doctor," cried a poor millionnaire in his agony. But no; the chink of coin is not musical in the ears of the Angel of death—the doom is pronounced, the judgment must proceed. Naked came you forth into life, naked must you return to death. Let poor men's blessings cluster round you, then, like a white cloud of angels; let fair robes of mercy and charity be your divine array. The Lord of heaven, the poor man's defender and keeper, will crown your head with a diadem of honour, and repay the deeds of Christ-like charity which you have done for Him with rich interest through eternity. *" Come, ye blessed of My Father, inherit the kingdom prepared for you from before the foundation of the world."*

X.

THE GOLDEN AUTUMN.

" So the Lord blessed the latter end of Job more than his beginning."—Job xlii. 12.

The young find something sad in the tints and skies of autumn; but as we grow older we love it better. There is that which is not out of tune with the colder flow of our own life currents, in the soft gray evening of the year. There is a certain quiet and hush in nature, when the stir of her spring and the toil of her summer are ended. A sigh of peace that so much is joyfully though painfully finished, seems to prolong itself through autumn. The world has no business then to trouble it; its noisy concerns are ended for the year. The groaning harvest has been gathered, and loads the portly barns; the fields lie bare and quiet, resting under the smile of heaven, and drinking in strength for new motherly cares and toils. I suppose it is this calm undertone of preparation and hope which makes autumn far from sad, to those who observe the reverse as well as the obverse of all the medals of nature and of life. The gray skies, the falling leaves, the whirling storms, the damps and mists of autumn, offer themselves to every eye, and to those whose eye is still the main inlet of impression they make the "fall" the dull, sad season of the year. But nature, at any rate, is not in despair about it; and those who have an eye for the quiet touches in nature's countenance, and an ear for the undertones of her song, catch somewhat of the inspiration of the hope which gladdens her while all is dying, and enter into her peace.

In truth she passes with something like triumphal pomp into her wintry tomb. She gathers her bravest mantle grandly around her as she falls. Just as the pomp of the sunset clouds robs nightfall of its terror, and prophesies over the death of day the glorious glow that will soon be tinting the eastern chambers, whence it will burst forth as a bridegroom, with a flush of triumph; so the year gathers a dress of living splendour around her, as her step grows tremulous, and the snows build the tomb which is to receive her to her winter sleep. There is a quiet, a grand, even a solemn tone about the hues and the expression of autumn, which have no depression in them, because no death. "*I shall not die, but live, and declare Thy wondrous works,*" nature is ever crying. "The king is dead; long live the king!" is the proclamation which they make on high over the graves of the years.

Life has its hum even in the dead hush of a midsummer noon. When the air seems so still that silence grows oppressive, lay your ear to the ground, and listen to the stir of the myriad insects that are keeping their summer festival. You will not marvel that simple hearts, in the good old times, believed that the grasses and the flower-cups were haunted, and that all the earth and air was thronged with troops of joyous invisible sprites, dancing in the sunbeams, swinging in the gossamer chains, hiding in the flower bells, and making the summer air musical with the breath of their merriment and song. It needs a more trained and observant ear to catch the same undertone through the sighing winds and swirling leaves of autumn, but it is there; life has but drawn back to its source awhile, and there it is gathering up its forces, renewing its youth, and preparing for the outburst of the spring. It is the sense that there is no death in nature, that she but weaves the dress of Him who ever liveth, and has commission to weave on while He liveth, which robs the autumn and the deepening winter of all but a passing breath of sadness, and makes their twilight hour the season of our most peaceful and happy musings. We too, if we have caught the divine key-note, are content to rest with them when the main toil of our life-work is over; to rest and ripen, and lay up in the inner cells the sap which shall make the flowers of our eternal spring. Sometimes, as in the Indian summer of Canada, and the St. Martin's summer of Switzerland, autumn has a glory of its own which contends with midsummer for the crown. Nature is never more splendid than in the calm golden sunset of such seasons as these; and then, too, the vine, noblest of all fruits, and needing noblest culture, yields her blushing juices, and prolongs far on towards the winter the living verdure and beauty of the year. And men celebrate "Advent" in midwinter. As the shadows lengthen and the world settles to its winter's sleep, homes grow glad; the long winter evenings are the seasons of family intercourse and the higher human joys. Not without significance is it that the great Advent festival is celebrated when nature lies bare and cold. There is in man's life a perpetual effort to realise that the spring of his hopes and joys lies where nature cannot touch it; that it is fed from a deeper fountain, which flows not with her floods, and ebbs not with her decline. The advent of Him who is our life, the world's life, we chiefly hail when all lies dead and cold around us; sign to us of a life which shall outlast the wreck of nature, and flourish in immortal youth when the earth has settled into the silence of its last winter; though earth, too, comes forth, quickened by the breath which quickens man, into the brightness of an eternal spring. When nature has spent all her substance and is beggared for the time, man opens his richer treasures, and brings forth his most precious stores. Life never seems so rich, so joyous, so boundless in promise, in hope, as when the home circle gathers round the Christmas fire, whose light flashes cheerily on the bleak wintry air; while laughter, song, and softer whispers, seem to mock the moaning wind, and exult joyously over decay and death.

My subject here is the autumn of life. A golden autumn, we all may make it, and then it is among the most beautiful, yea, the most fruitful, of all the seasons of life.

I. The key to the beauty of autumn must be sought in the coming spring.

"*At even time there shall be light,*" is the broad grand promise which stretches like a heaven of brightness over this world of struggle, decay, and death. Evening is lit by the promise of morning, autumn is lit by the promise of spring; and life's quiet eventide is lit by the radiance of the eternal heaven. Strike out that promise, kill the germ that lies in the heart of decay, the hope that nestles and stirs under the ribs of death, and the world is a huge sepulchre—a chamber of horrors, where all loathsome things are gathered, and souls go shuddering by. But God hath writ the promise large, so that every eye can read it—"*light at evening time.*" To every brave effort, to every high hope, to every strong endurance, to every weary day of toil, there is light at evening; because, to those who have the heart to look for them, behind the gathering gloom there is God, heaven, and eternity. Nothing that lives need dread the darkness; to the living it is but the veil of a brighter day.

And here is the inspiration of life in its decline, an inspiration which may make its decline more beautiful, more hopeful, than its spring. At the root of all that can ennoble and beautify the wasting decaying powers, lies the love of God and the hope of heaven. Let a man open his heart in his spring to that fountain of renewing, let him plant himself early by the watercourses of God's grace and love, and he robs the destroyer of all his power and all his terror. The decay which touches his life as a creature, and begins to wither and waste his powers the moment he has touched his prime—the eclipse which falls over nature as the ear grows dull, and the eye grows dim, are but the wearing out of a dress which has served him awhile; he watches, not calmly only, but with quiet thankfulness, as it grows thin and drops piecemeal into dust, longing to put on the braver dress which he will wear in the presence-chamber of the King of kings.

Give a man love and hope, and what can sadden him? Love for the present, hope for the future, a spring of pure fresh joy which can never fail him, a glow in the distance hourly brightening, which, as he nears it, flashes out into glorious day. If men nourished their souls more freely at these fountains, and breathed more deeply these inspirations, should we hear so much, think you, of sour, crabbed, and querulous old age? What makes men sour and crabbed, but because their roots so rarely touch the everlasting river? What makes men querulous, but because they cloud with their vanity and selfishness the flush in the skies of hope? I have known one of splendid power of intellect and spirit, full of the energy that can lead and govern men, made as feeble as an infant, as dependent, by the first touch of advancing death; and he spent long helpless months, nay years, in the calmest acquiescence, the serenest peace, the most cheerful contentment with the Higher Will to which his life had been one long homage, in the most gentle, nay, playful self-adjustment to the new, and to the onlookers, sad conditions of the strong man's long decay. So also have I seen a smile more beautiful than any which I have seen in living faces, playing around a dead man's lips.

Feed your spring and summer in the green pastures, and at the still waters by which the Eternal Shepherd is ever striving to lead you; grapple your heart of hearts to the Friend whose fellowship, whose love, shall be like the springs and the palms of Elim to the panting and fainting host, and then fear not but that the autumn of your life, however storm-beaten and bare, will have a golden beauty of its own, which will leave no regrets for summer, and which will have closer kindred with the radiant glory of eternity.

I have said of old age, dwelling on the aspect which it so constantly and so sadly wears in such a world as this, that the main work and interest of life is over when the children go forth and leave the parents in the old home alone. It is true enough in a sense. From that time the day begins to draw downwards, the shadows lengthen, and there is a chill in the evening air that flavours of night. It is much as moonlight to sunlight, this age of life to which the grandchild belongs rather than the child. The age when the stir and struggle of the battle are over, when the business is made, and the position is won, and the busy and burdensome part of it passes into younger and more energetic hands. But the moonlight has its beauty as well as the sunlight, and it is richer in suggestions of the spiritual and heavenly sphere. And God is very tender with us. I am often full of wonder at the tender fatherly touches that lie thick about us in all the order and conduct of our lives. How few homes are stript quite bare; how few aged ones are left quite alone! How constantly love, prompted of God, makes some tender provision for their quiet evening and darkening night! One daughter stays by them perhaps, or a niece, a grandchild, a ward, who finds it a dear and sacred duty to cheer and smooth their down-hill path, and who makes the otherwise desolate home beautiful and blessed by the ministries of devoted and vigilant love.

And if all the young ones are gone, " John Anderson," and his dear old dame, are not the saddest figures upon earth, as they live over the past again by their " ain fireside," or tread together the shortening path; and when one goes first, the other is not long in following—God will not keep them too far or too long apart. There is a cloud, and to the eye of sense it looks a dark and a dense one, overshadowing the age of decay and decrepitude; but we can catch the edge of the silver lining and see a soft fair lustre lighting the path to the very borders of the tomb. There it brightens with an awful brightness:

> " To death it is given,
> To see how this earth lies embosomed in heaven."

II. To prepare for a golden fruitful autumn should be one of the main aims of a man in his youth and his prime.

Not that our chief work here is to prepare for times and seasons, save as far as the preparation for one time is the preparation for all time. There is no schism in the body of our times. Man is one, and his life is one, through all its stages; and there is nothing better for the child, for the youth, for the man, for the old man, for the dying man, than "*to do justly, to love mercy, and to walk humbly with his God.*" There is nothing which can prepare a man for the peaceful and fruitful autumn of life, which will not equally be his preparation for the winter of death, and the spring of resurrection. But the thought of the years of decline and decay which are before him, "*ere yet the silver cord be loosed, or the golden bowl be broken, or the mourners go about the streets;*" when, if he have no springs within which are fed from the perennial spring on high, life will be but a long and terrible wrestling with death, may well drive in on a man's heart and conscience the lesson, "*Remember now thy Creator in the days of thy youth,*" and inspire the prayer, "Let me live the life of the righteous, that my last end may be like theirs."

There are few men who do not think anxiously about some provision for the evening of life, when the powers will be feebler for their tasks, and the hope of rest from the toils of business will grow daily more dear. Men will save and pinch, and starve their children's minds at any rate, if not their bodies, to lay up gold against the days of decline and decay. A provision for old age is one of the main inspirations of the years of business toils and cares. "There is another thousand safe against the time when I can work no longer," a man says to himself, and finds in the thought a rich compensation for many privations and for wearing toils. *But wherefore spend ye your money for that which is not bread? and your labour for that which satisfieth not?* An old age with plenty to feed it, and nothing to occupy, interest, and cultivate it, is surely one of the most dismal things under the sun. I would have you prepare a real and rich provision—bread and wine that will make your age fairer and fresher than your youth, which will make your home a nook to which young children love to gather, as bees cluster to flowers, to sip the nectar of your wisdom, and nestle in the embrace of your love.

Nor do I mean by these counsels to urge you to what would be called " the exclusive cultivation of piety." It is a great mistake to suppose that God can dispense with the cultivation of any of our powers. The man who systematically lets mind and body go to wreck, while he cares exclusively for what he pleases to consider " the interests of his soul," is in a fair way to spend a joyless and loveless old age, and to lie at length in a forgotten tomb. Piety is only seen in its true strength and beauty in the harmony of all the powers. It sits as queen, but it is cheerless and joyless without its court. A cleanly, pure, robust body; a cultivated, well-stored, and penetrating mind; a large, tender, and sympathetic heart, as well as a pious believing spirit, go to make old age honoured and blest.

And I would have young men remember, in view of the infirmities and sorrows of age, that a wasteful and wanton youth, makes the chief of the blots which disfigure, and the pains which torment it. If you want years of miserable decay, begin early to "live fast." It is a sure receipt. It is sin, as I have said, which lends all that is terrible to decay and death. But for the work of sin in us, the work of time upon us would be benign and beautiful as on the "green bay-tree," whose leaves wither and drop only when they are thrust out by the buds of spring. And excess in youth, excess of all sorts, leaves its bitter and inevitable legacy, in a fretful, weary, hateful old age. When I speak of excess, I am not simply thinking of the coarser forms; girls in their vanities, frivolities, and dissipations, may be as wasteful of the vital energy as men in their gambling dens and stews. You reckon so much saved each day to make your old age "warm," as the saying goes. I wish you would open a larger ledger, and reckon that the manful conquest of a temptation to vicious indulgence, the curtailment of a wasteful amusement or pursuit, the effort to expand the physical powers with which God has endowed you, that you may keep a sound body to be the tabernacle of a sound mind, itself to be cultivated by other discipline, is a far nobler and a far more useful investment, and one that will pay better in the common stuff of comfort and happiness, than untold stores of gold. Paralysis is little the better for gilding. A bleared eye and a shaky hand get but little pleasure out of rolls of crisp bank-notes. And youth is the time to practise the lesson. "Oh, could I but have my youth over again!" how many palsied reprobates are crying. For remember, young friends, a constitution once impaired, health once broken, vital strength once squandered, no agony of effort, or even prayer, can repair or restore.

I would counsel all men and women, and more especially those of constant and close occupation, during their days of enterprise and energy, when the whole time and strength seems to be imperiously demanded for the day's work, to set apart some small fragment of them rigidly, as consecrated to yet higher use. I say yet higher use. For I regard the honourable toils of business, or of the home management, as a very high and worthy use of the powers. I would have men throw their energy into commerce, as into a work which is worthy of them; and I would have women master the details of home economy with a thoroughness which would leave their servants but little independent scope. Figures, stuffs, bills —it may seem poor in detail, but it is not a poor thing to help to carry on, however humbly, the great commerce of life. By these things the world lives and grows, and offers an ever-widening seed-field to him who has the seed of the divine culture to cast into it, fresh from the Great Sower's hand.

But much of the cheerfulness and happiness of life's autumn, depend on the measure in which a man has concerned himself with something other than his business, with the culture of the intellect, the enlargement of the higher faculties of the being, and their education for a superior sphere. How many men when they relax the strain of attention to business, and women when the children are married, and the main part of their home cares is off their hands, begin at once to stagnate—happy if they do not become like sluggish waters, foul with weeds and slime. Men who will not read when they are young, cannot read when they are old. They have no interest in it, and no heart for it. Men who will not go forth into nature, and train themselves to search into her wonders, while their minds and senses are keen, when they grow old sit moping over their fires, or go pottering about their gardens, killing the most precious thing in the universe to the wise man—time, time to think, time to acquire, time to love, time to bless mankind.

But there are men of business, who are not

indisposed to cultivate their minds, and lay up some priceless stores of thoughts and habits to cheer the evening of their days, who yet complain that they have not a moment for study or even for a look at nature; business presses morning, noon, and night, and must be done. Well, the root of it all is "hasting to be rich," to put it in plain terms. You cannot get rich while you are young, and give at the same time some fair cultivation to your nobler powers. Be absorbed, body, soul, and spirit, in business, and life becomes a business; and when you are out of business, you have no business at all in life.

I would have every man of close occupation make it a sacred duty to keep up a living knowledge of, and interest in, some pursuit, science, art, or craft, outside the circle of his daily task. Thereby he will keep his mental faculties in fair play upon their appointed objects, and lay up for himself a pursuit and an education, which will occupy nobly and happily the autumn of life. What men want is something to carry on their education till they die—something which will continually draw them out to fresh observation, fresh reflection, fresh acquisition, with ever stronger and riper power. And such objects must be set before the mind's eye in youth, they must give their tincture to the blood when it is warm and vivid. No middle-aged man can hope to break up a new seedfield of thought with any chance of a high success. Clip a bit from your daily earnings rather than from your daily study. Surround yourselves with objects of interest and beauty, the mere living with which will be a partial education, preparing you to search out their more hidden meanings, when the toil of your busiest years is over, and you can spare time and thought for the things which your soul has taught itself to delight in and to love.

How many of your friends seem to be enlarging, ripening, and rising heavenward with the years? Cold, hard, selfish, loveless old age abounds; mainly because men sell so much of the pith and the fire of their youth for gold, and are just like a worked-out mine of force, when the life of earth should be ripening for heaven. The play and even the strain of the faculties—the various faculties of body, mind, and spirit, in wise proportions and alternations—is the true human joy. Plenty to think of, plenty to observe, plenty to pursue, plenty to delight in, plenty to help, plenty to love—these make the gladness and the riches of the being. And men and women who deliberately shut themselves up to a narrow pasture, and care just for one thing in life, the business or the household toils, spend a joyless spring, a sunless summer, quite miss their autumn, and settle into the drearihood of winter in their prime. It is said of some nations that they know no childhood, the children become little men and women as soon as they can flirt and strut. Equally sad is it for a people to have no benign and rich old age. And it is just the goodness and manifoldness of the objects with which a man occupies himself in his prime, the objects of his thought, pursuit, and love through his spring and summer, which make his autumn golden, and shield its fruits from the blights of winter, till they are gathered into the garners on high.

III. The occupations and cares of a golden autumn have a larger scope and richer interest, though they may be inspired by a feebler energy, than those of the youth and the prime. For—

1. The head ought to grow wiser as the hands grow feebler and the pulse slower. The man whose busy life is well-nigh done, has a noble sphere in counselling the workers, and tempering

in due measures the fervour of youth with the calmness, the certainty, and the constancy of age. In due measures, I say, and here is where the old seem so constantly to fail, and to throw themselves out of gear with the new times. They fight against the current instead of striking in with it, and lose all power of guiding it, in the hopeless, desperate endeavour to stem it or to turn it aside. For stemmed it will not be, aside it will not go. Each age has its new key-note. There are but few of the aged who seem able to catch the tune of the new time, and to strike in with it. The ways, the habits, the needs, the aims, the hopes, of the young generation jar on them. It sounds like a new gospel, and anathema is ready on their lips. And the young delight to parade its newness. They take pride in the new time and in its promise, and flout the wisdom of the past. Yet the new time is much more like the old time, young friends, than you are dreaming; the thoughts that stir your blood, stirred your fathers' before you were born. But if the old-men, instead of looking lovingly upon the new ideas and methods which the young energy of the age invents or announces, and the ardent hope with which it starts on its career, will frown, and carp, and sneer, will obstruct enterprises and prophecy miscarriages, will seek to lower the tone of effort, and to chill the ardour of hope, they will be driven to the wall inevitably; the tides may be stopped as easily as the progress of the times. I would that old men could believe more heartily in God as the leader of the progress, and be sure that the new age, equally with the old, is under His guiding hand. If they find it hard to trust it, at least let them trust the God who leads it, and show a genial joy in its progress, for it does but continue the progress which in their times they led.

Above all, I would have the young impetuous spirits believe that their fathers have pored over the same problems which puzzle them, and have tried in their way the solutions of which the new time makes its boasts. They have made no great discovery, however brilliant may be their speculations; they simply stand on the vantage ground of their fathers' lives, and sweep the horizon of a somewhat wider world. I would have them soften, in their intercourse with the elders, the contrasts which they are prone to exaggerate, and bring forth the common truth which underlies the conflicting statements, delighting to recognise the bond which makes the first and the last generations one. I would have them honour the battle-cries which the fathers bore through many a hard-fought field of intellectual and spiritual conflict, and take their chief joy and pride in that which unites them with the past. We should have less schism then in homes and generations, and the old would be less disposed to moan that God keeps them lingering on ground which they seem but to cumber, and that the world would get on better, and would escape many sorrows and troubles, if they were fairly out of the way.

But the true old man's wisdom needs no such pliances and concessions. It will blend kindly with the young enthusiasm; it will guide and temper it; it will lend it method and firmness, and show to it the way to realise its hope. The old man's chair ought to be the oracle to the young ones of the household, the company, the state. They should be drawn to his wisdom as stars to their sun. The gray-headed patriarch, if he understands the secret of his power, if he grows while he lives, will make his word a more powerful, and his work a more precious thing, than when he could throw into them all the fire and energy of his youth. A wise and genial old man or woman is one of the noblest of human figures, if not the very noblest. There is something in the true relation of the patriarch to the younger race growing up under his shadow, at which we have just hinted, which is singularly beautiful. But for selfishness—selfish old men, selfish young men—we should realise it as a principle of divine order in all our homes and states. The quiet withdrawing from the scenes of hot and contentious activity which occupy the prime of every life, should be but the beginning of a new and calmer, but a more constant, benign, and noble energy; of which the home circle, the business, the parish, the state, according to the sphere and the habit of the life, should show blessed and abundant fruits. And this leads us to a second point.

2. One of the main concerns of a life in its golden autumn is charity.

I use the word in its larger sense. I would include in it all that disciplined, patient, unselfish energy can do to serve mankind, and most especially the afflicted of this world and its poor. To wise, good men, in their golden autumn, society looks to be its almoners, its guardians, its overseers. Rising above the narrow interests of a business which has gain for its inspiration, they find a wider, nobler field before them in the service of their fellow-men. "The cause that we know not," like Job, they can "search out for us." They can be "eyes to the blind, and feet to the lame;" they can be "fathers to the poor;" they can "break for us the jaws of the wicked, and pluck the spoil out of their teeth." The wisdom, the patience, the compassion which they have gained in the battle, they can exercise for us in a nobler field. They can be the elders of our churches, the guardians of our poor, the visitors of our prisoners and captives, the nurses of our sick, the teachers of our ignorant, the guides of our public and private ministries of mercy. Their old age may be more than beautiful; the golden autumn may glow into glory. There have been men and women in their green old age, with no transcendent powers, who have made themselves names as angels of mercy, which shall ring through the world while the world endures.

There is thus a large sphere of duty, and that the highest, which they may make all their own; in which no young, brilliant Elihu can compete with them. And they may so occupy it that, when the tottering limbs fail at last, and refuse to bear the still eager spirit through its wonted rounds, it shall bring poor men's blessings round their dying pillow, thick as the troop of white-winged angels, who wait to bear the worn-out soldier of duty from his field of battle to his glorious rest. I think that in God's scheme of our lives, which our selfishness is ever marring, but of which in the lives of our greatest and purest we have gleams, this season of higher service is interposed with benign beauty between the busy and too selfish cares of our maturity, and the yet higher service in God's kingdom to which it is to exalt us beyond.

3. The golden autumn of life ought to be a quiet but profoundly impressive homily upon hope.

Quiet, I say. The evening does not babble about the morrow. The autumn does not babble about the spring. "*In quietness and confidence shall be your strength*" is the patriarch's text. Quiet trust, quiet joy, quiet hope. We are almost losing our knowledge of the quiet virtues. Old age, ripe and genial, with a glow still on it, must keep them before our sight. I would not have the patriarchs always talking about heaven. "Pious talk," from lips or from books, has done its utmost to mar the witness of pious life. Little talk there may be, though words on heaven fall sweetly from aged lips, but I would have old men look as if they were familiar with its pathways, and not without some rich foretaste of its joys.

The fixed expression of their gentle decline should be hope. Men catch it readily enough, and feel the inspiration of it, when it is there. I am not sure that it was not the unconscious contagion of the strange joy and hope with which the apostolic Church was animated, which commenced the revival that swept with its quickening breath through all the higher philosophy and literature of the pagan world. Hope is a gospel which life really preaches. And children even can see when decay and death are stripped of their terrors, and when the beloved and honoured elders in their home, just

> "Long for evening to undress,
> That they may rest with God."

Nothing, I am sure, strikes such a pure, high key-note in a home, as an old age which has a genial smile for earth, and a home-longing look to heaven. And forms of dear and honoured patriarchs come up into my memory as I write these words, grand and good old men, to live under the shadow of whose lives was a benediction, and who have left households rich in reverence, rich in concord, rich in hope. God send to us old age so full of tender, childlike interest in all human things, that infants may prattle their tales into its ear; so full of ripe wisdom and celestial love, that angels might find in it fit audience for the histories and the hymns of heaven! The beautiful link of the two worlds! Strong, brave father! Wise, true mother! The frame is bowed a little, and the step grows tremulous. There are wrinkles on the broad, calm brow, and the clear pallor of healthy age tones the once ruddy cheek. The enemy has his touch on you, but a smile steals up as you recognise the form which brings your summons to your home, your rest. The last legacy, I think, which you will leave to your children, and your children's children, when you part from them, will be the smile of immortal life, playing around the stiffening lips of death.

XI.

THE WHOLE FAMILY.

"*The whole family.*"—Eph. iii. 15.

To comprehend this wholeness we must take in the two worlds. Life completes itself through death. By death only the two bands whom death had severed become one. And this is the Christian victory over death. The terror compelled to become the minister; the demon transformed into the angel; the great destroyer changed into the great reconciler, and constrained to complete with eternal perfectness that unity which, but for Christ, he had for ever destroyed.

I cling to the thought of "over-abounding grace" which fills so large a space in the writings of St. Paul. Words have to stretch themselves to their utmost tension, to express what the apostle realised when he meditated on the divine mystery, "*The love of God in Christ, which passeth* knowledge." "*Moreover, the law entered that the offence might abound; but where sin abounded, grace did much more abound; that as sin hath reigned unto death, even so might grace reign, through righteousness, unto eternal life, by Jesus Christ our Lord.*" The contrast between "abounded" and "much more abounded," in our translation, very poorly expresses the force of the contrast in the original expression of St. Paul. Not a superior but a superlative mastery is expressed by his impetuous words. Grace shall not rebuild ruins only, but recreate with superlative grandeur and splendour what sin had destroyed; and foremost among these transformations is this transformation of death. Death through Christ completes the edifice of life, and crowns it. The touch which, through the legacy which Adam left us, rifles homes and hearts of their treasures, in Christ becomes their consecration; the dew of death is transmuted into the chrism of eternal joy.

"O death, I will be thy plagues! O grave, I will be thy destruction!" cried the prophet in the Divine name, under a dispensation which we too readily believe saw through the veil but dimly, and had but feeble grasp of the realities of "life and immortality." It is just this triumphant sense of power over the dark element in life—over all that belongs to the region of the shadow of death—which the gospel of life substantiates. Such passages as these in the Old Testament scripture—and they are many—are the first notes of the exulting strain which runs through the New, and finds fullest expression in the rapturous language of St. Paul. Words cannot express the sense of exuberant power which filled him, when he realised what his life as a redeemed man in Christ implied and prophesied. All the sadness of life, all the bitterness of death, absolutely vanished from his field of vision. Was tribulation his experience, "*bonds, afflictions, persecutions,*" a glorious joy possessed him, and bore him through them triumphantly. Did death affront him, and there was no moment when it was far away, he but lifted his voice in a more joyous burst of thanksgiving, that death was for ever "*swallowed up in victory.*"

What timid reading do we give to the words, "*If while we were enemies we were reconciled to God by the death of His Son, much more, being reconciled, we shall be saved by His life!*" If the death destroyed death for us, and wrought our great deliverance, how much more shall the life enrich and glorify life! Have faith, and exult in the boundless possibilities of the future. "*Said I not unto thee that if thou wouldest believe, thou shouldest see the glory of God?*" Does any one of us imagine, even faintly, what that may mean? Is it a brother restored on earth to a dear embrace —the light shining again in the home, with a tinge in it of celestial brightness, as the risen man, recovered from death, rejoined the familiar company? Or is it the brothers gathering in the eternal home, purged of all stain, and pure from every taint and flaw, bathed in the lustre of the supernal sunlight, one in love, in life, for evermore? A strange and awful joy, surely, shall possess us, when we behold once more the parted, and miss for ever the mortal blemish, the flaws, the stains, the weaknesses of sin, and see the noble features which we loved and cherished transfigured, bright with an immortal beauty, and glowing with an immortal life. We shall have a vision then of what "*saved by His life*" may mean. Till then, "*Lord, we believe; but help Thou our unbelief.*"

Let me ask you to consider with me—

I. The inevitable rupture of the unity of the home.

We say not, it *may be* broken: it must be broken. The hour comes inevitably when you shall watch the death-shadow deepening on the face that you most dearly love. The last word will be spoken, the last look of love will gleam forth, and then you question the still rosy lips, but they are for ever silent; you search the depths of the beloved eyes, but a film has gathered over them, the depths have vanished, only a cold dull mask is there. And a great agony seizes the soul that is widowed; a great wail, a great appeal, it may be a great protest, goes up from an overstrained heart to God. This lies in the future of every home, blessed be God. We say blessed be God in *faith* here, we shall repeat it in open vision there, when death has transplanted the whole family to the home which the Lord has founded and adorned for it on high. But a stern, sad experience lies between all of us and that consummation; an experience which the steadfast vision of the consummation alone can transmute into solemn and holy joy.

And Death, who bursts the bond and rifles the treasures of our homes, wears to the eye of sense no angelic aspect. In this sin-haunted sphere he still wears his dress of terrors. He is one of God's chief preachers of righteousness, and bears a form which drives his lessons home. Were death but translation, we could hail his advent. Enoch, Elijah, found death, the one a gentle, the other a triumphant passage, to the joys and the splendours of eternity. But Adam left not translation as his legacy to his children. "*Sin entered into the world, and death by sin,*" and death, wedded to sin, brought a terror of dying into the human heart. Part of death, perhaps the saddest part, is the inevitable decay; the long, slow, sad decline, sad but for the light which falls on it from a higher sphere. "*As our outer man decayeth, our inner man is renewed day by day.*" "*For we know, that, if our earthly house of this tabernacle were dissolved, we have a building of God, a house not made with hands, eternal in the heavens. For in this we groan, earnestly desiring to be clothed upon with our house which is from heaven: if so be that being clothed, we shall not be found naked. For we that are in this tabernacle do groan, being burdened: not for that we would be unclothed, but clothed upon, that mortality might be swallowed up of life*" (2 Cor. v. 1–4).

God will not have us forget in this world the evil tree, of which sin is the bitter fruit. All the dread apparatus of death, is God's lesson to the living about sin. There is no attempt on the part of heaven to soften or sweeten the homily. Christianity brought to us no mitigation of the physical pains and fears of dying. Its whole work is in the spirit which endures them, and sees in them the birth-pangs of the life eternal. And this is the solace, yea, the more than solace, of bereavement in a Christian home: the whole family, limb by limb, and organ by organ, is being born into the home where it shall dwell eternally.

A touch of sadness must enter here into all our loves. The closer we twine the heart-strings, the sharper the pain when they part, as part they must. It is the dire necessity of life—death, and the heart-aches, the life weariness that death brings in its train. The family stock lives on, but the old leaves drop and the young buds expand and occupy their room, to wither and die in turn. Not only has Christianity not mitigated the physical pain and the fear that attend on death, there is a sense in which it has intensified them. There can be no question that the influence of the gospel has raised to a higher pitch our joys and hopes. The sensibilities of humanity have grown more keen, the bonds have been drawn more close in homes and states. Human joy is a higher thing, purer and more intense, since the day when one could say in the name of Christ, "*Rejoice in the Lord alway, and again I say rejoice;*" but with intenser joy, also, intenser pain. The larger body casts the larger shadow, and as humanity has grown in strength, dignity, and conception of what life means and life is worth, the pains and the fears have grown with it; there is more at stake, more to lose, more to suffer.

And this has been the work of the gospel. It has taught us how to love. It has dignified, purified, and consecrated the most intense of the forms of love. It has made wedded love a loftier thing than anything of which a pagan dreamed; and it has added fresh strength and tenderness to the relationships which grow out of the home. But it is not afraid of increasing in the circle of light, lest it should increase also the circumference of shadow. It is not afraid of exalting the joys of life, because its pain must grow more intense by the same rule; for it holds that life and joy are the conquerors. Darkness and pain are for time, light and joy are for eternity. In strengthening the life, the love, it is giving to us an eternal victory. It bids us front the peril, and smile at the pain, from which it cannot shield us, because of its abounding power to bear us through it and beyond it; and to complete our life in the world where there shall be no more pain for ever. In the home life the double experience is realised most intensely. The Christian home makes most of its relationships, and the gap is widest, the pain is deepest, when the circle is broken in upon by death. But the Christian household aims at a higher completeness than the life of this world can compass. It is not an accident, it is not a stroke, it is a vital stage of its growth, it is a grand step of its progress toward its consummation, when its dearest pass through the veil and beckon the mourners from beyond. For—

II. The whole family, death only can complete.

Death has a double aspect, as he works through Christ or through Adam. In the one he despoils, in the other he crowns us; in the one he disrobes, in the other he arrays us; in the one he breaks up the unity, which in the other he completes. Wholeness belongs not to this world. There is no whole human experience, there is no whole human friendship, there is no whole human possession, which is all contained within this world's bounds. I have endeavoured in a former discourse to prove to you how man must take the eternal into his horizon of vision, if he is to understand truly even a fragment of his present life. Like some cunning royal texture, where there is a peculiar thread running through the whole fabric, so that the smallest portion tells the tale of the place and year of its production, there is not a broken bit of the most wasted life which has not some feature about it that can be explained only by eternity. And if we can say it of the basest fragment, must we not believe of the noblest fabric which the Lord has founded and edified in this world, that it too has an eternal life, which can be seen in its completeness only "*in the general assembly and Church of the first-born*" on high. The family which we see, that portion of it which earth contains at any moment, is but a ring, a link of a golden chain, which is dropped from heaven and taken up into heaven again.

Children of a Christian home, it is sacred ground on which you are standing, it has been won for you by the toils, the heroisms, the sacrifices, perhaps by the life-blood of godly sires. That family tradition, that atmosphere of the family life, in which you were nurtured, which you breathed with your first breath, and which has lent its tincture from the first to the currents of your blood, was not the creature of accident or even of words. How many noble lives of men and women do you reckon in your line? How many names are in your family Bibles which are also written in the Lamb's book of life? Step by step, perhaps generation by generation, the family has lifted itself to a higher level, has attained to a wider culture, and has taken a larger part in the affairs of life. Who shall tell what brave struggles, heroic endurances, wrestling prayers, utter sacrifices, have made that fabric of the family life and the family fortunes, which are your rich inheritance? And what is left of them— these men and women whose sacred dust is your vantage ground, and whose achievements are your heritage? Is it simply that dust and those sacred memories? Is a memory of them all that lives in God's universe? And when you die, is a memory all that will survive of you? It was for you, for their children's children, that these men toiled and suffered; that the *family* might live before

God, they watched, and wept, and prayed. They are gone, but have they borne no loves and visions with them; loves that cling still to the dear ones who hold the legacy of their lives, and visions of the time, when they shall see of their travail as the children join them, and gather the fruit of their toils in eternity?

Surely there is something in this family stock which has a real existence in the universe. It is not a name only, a string on which a succession of individuals may be strung, and wear the appearance of a unity. It is real and not nominal, a thing and not a name. A thing which has a clear existence before the eye of God, and which will have the substance, as well as wear the appearance, of a unity in eternity. There is a whole family life, of which each individual, and even each generation, is but a section. It has a distinct form, a type of feature, a character, and a mission in the world. It would startle us to see how much the essential characteristics of families, running through and tinging the diverse members, tell as a distinct and powerful element upon the development of society. If the family is to nurse the individual man to his complete maturity, it is that he may continue and carry out the influence of the family life. Each man's work in his household is to live out with full freedom the special capacity for life which is in him; that belongs partly to him and partly to his race. That race is a reality before God in its wholeness; it has a speciality of gift and function, and a work in the world which it only can fulfil. We *see* this on a grand scale in the character and the mission of nations, but it runs through the whole race. The man and his belongings, his father's fathers and his children's children, form a whole which enters as a factor into the order of God's everlasting kingdom. The bond of the household is not accidental and for time, it is essential and for eternity.

And the treasures which a home life, such as I have striven to picture, gathers, are not treasures of this world that can perish in its wreck; they have the mint-mark of heaven on them—they must pass up and appear on high. The infant in the home seems to be the poorest and most helpless of creatures under the sun; poor in power, but rich in right, and rich in love. As it grows it gathers its riches round it. The work of life is to lay them up in sure storehouses, "*where moth and rust corrupt not, and thieves break not through to steal."* The child learns to lay its hands on the things that are needful for the nurture and culture of the being, and to lay the clasp of its heart on persons whose love it demands by those sure instincts which never fail. Trace childhood on to its maturity. The man or the woman of fifty have made themselves a name and a place in life; they are the centres of attraction to troops of friends; they have sons and daughters growing up in their homes, who pay to them the reverent obedience which they pay to the Father God. They have furnished their minds with knowledge, the universe has unveiled its secrets, the past is peopled with heroic forms, the future with visions which the eye of faith alone is strong enough to behold. How rich life has become to them, how full its storehouses of knowledge, power, and love! Trace it a stage further. At seventy, the puling, helpless, portionless infant has grown into a patriarch, whose white hairs are a crown of honour, before which all men joyfully bow. The sons and daughters have each made themselves a home, and little infants, of whom he has all the joy and none of the care, come climbing round his knee, and twine soft tendrils round the boughs of his strength; lending to his age the grace and the charm of youth once more. His wisdom has grown ripe with large experience, his affections and sympathies wide with frequent ministries; he fills the place of a prince in his circle, and when he falls a wide company of men feels beggared awhile by his loss.

And what does his fall mean? What but that a larger and loftier home circle has need of him, that the wise and the good who have gone on before are waiting to welcome him to their fellowship, to lead his disciplined and ripened power to the work for which God was training it, and to rest his heart in the home-life of heaven. The rich experience of which the home-life of earth had been the parent, would make the heavenly life strange, and even foreign, if the home did not reappear beyond the river. The man who has been nursed to a noble maturity by such fellowship as we have been describing, would find the higher life an exile, if "home" were not the essential form of its relationships, if love, the love of kindred souls, and the intercourse which it generates, were not the essential principle of its life. The patriarch of the earthly home, passes out of it to be joined to the patriarchal company —" the spirits of just men made perfect," whose home-life but perpetuates in heavenly forms all that was best and dearest in his mortal pilgrimage. And there too the infants, "the flowers that grow between," whom the Angel bears early home, find loving nurses; there is tender training for the young immortals in a home where love rules all the sphere.

I have firm belief in the specific uses of all the faculty that is cultured in this world, in the life of the world to come. This seems to me to be the meaning of the Apocalypse, of all the unveilings of the secrets of the heavenly life which the scripture affords. Its simple, honest homelikeness, to me is its broadest and most striking feature—the entire absence of strangeness in its objects, its interests, its joys. It may be said this presentation of it is a concession to the necessary imperfections and limitations of our knowledge: that the things unseen can only be represented by familiar images, if they are to carry any sense of realness to our human apprehension; and that the fact of the employment of these earthly images conveys no absolute truth about the eternal world. But there seems to me to be an underlying question, the settlement of which may modify our judgment—In a being like man, made in

God's own image, and made intelligent by God's own light, how far does the necessary use of these human images cast light for us on the nature of the realities which the Spirit employs them to set forth? The forms of things which man apprehends, are forms which God has shown to him; the question occurs, has God, so to speak, two sets of forms, essentially diverse, with which to occupy the intelligence of His child? Or is the one the key to the other, after the fashion of the Mount of Transfiguration; the body wearing its familiar likeness, yet aglow with the awful splendour of the celestial world?

I believe in the permanence of gifts and the perpetuity of culture. The artists, the thinkers, the seers, the statesmen, if through faith they gain right of entrance, will find the work waiting for them which they loved best, and were best trained for—their joyous task, their fruitful ministry to humanity through eternity. Men live in a rank here; it is the secret of the divine order of society; they belong to a race, they fall into a line. Dying in faith, they fall at once into a kindred rank in heaven. And there alone the wholeness of a life, of a home, of a line, can appear. It is here in segments, always the complete orb is hidden. The eye of faith may faintly trace its outline, as in the young moon on a clear summer night; but it can only appear, the whole orb illumined, when it moves with full face opposed to the Celestial Sun. And here we trace Death's loftiest ministry. This wholeness Death only can complete. In the Christian home death is the fulfilment of the highest and most eager of the heart's aspirations; the hand of God, adding to the beloved the touch of divine completeness, and lifting them to the home where the whole family will at length be one.

III. Very benign, too, very precious is the reflex action of this ministry of death on our home life here.

That He may bring heaven nearer to the following, he separates the two bands. Life never becomes earnest and sacred, as it was meant to be, until the shadow of death has fallen on it. Those only who have questioned the face of the beloved dead know what is meant by life. A family lives but a half life, until it has sent some whom it has clasped in its embrace to join the forerunners whose lives it inherits; until those whose work is still in this world, in spirit can cross the river, and fold beloved but transfigured forms to their hearts. Some shadow on earth's sunlight there must be, and the darkest of all shadows on a home is this shadow of death. No agony known to mortals can surpass, and but little can mate, the anguish of Eve, of Jacob, of David, of Mary, when their dearest lay dead. But behind it, within it, rather let us say, if we fear not to enter the cloud, lies the glory. "*Said I not unto thee, that if thou wouldest believe, thou shouldest see the glory of God?*"

And those who have been permitted to stand by the deathbed of a noble Christian disciple, who have seen him sustained and possessed by the powers of the world to come—the dying eye ranging on through the bounds of the world of sense, and lit by a gleam from some sphere which was beyond our sight; and then the light fading from the eye, and the face settling into the awful but beautiful serenity of death, till it put on the aspect of a warrior taking his rest on the breast of victory—have known a moment of sublime joy which has hardly fallen short of transport, and have gone down to the common world again, like Moses, with the lustre still on them, and with a sacred power to penetrate the inner sanctuaries of the hearts of their fellow-men.

Those most familiar with the higher aspects of death know most of the higher aspects of life. To them the common ground becomes sacred, for saints who are at rest with God have trodden it; the common duties become holy, for they mingle with the earthly, the thoughts and the energies of the heavenly sphere. And if God makes breaches in your home circle, understand the loving reason; it is that He may separate the *one* into *two* bands awhile, still declaring their oneness, and so may marry the two spheres. The little home that has sheltered you in its sunny nook has expanded. There is now but one home everywhere. Those who are "*bone of your bone and flesh of your flesh*" are treading the heavenly pathways. How often as you gaze longingly on yon fair star, do they cross the line of your sight! How lovingly will they welcome you, and efface all strangeness when you join them! Dear hands will one day lead you through the unaccustomed paths. The bringing you into the home, the home of the whole family, will be one of their most intense delights. They wait; they share the expectant attitude of the universe: God has prepared some better thing for all of us; they without us will not be made perfect.

The mother who has seen that awful pallor steal over the brow of her nursling, and the life flicker on the stiffening lips, knows then, and not till then, the sacredness of those who are left to her. She knows that she has to train them for two worlds—nay, for one, for that godly life which, whether here or there, is life eternal. Nor will the aged pilgrim, who has sent all his dearest on before him, tremble when he too stands on the brink of the river. His heart will be bursting with joy at the thought, "In a moment the veil will be lifted, it is trembling already, and my dead will be clasped to my heart again, to be parted no more for ever." The image of Rachel came back to Jacob as he stood on the shore of the dark rolling stream. It is very touching to note how the memories of her mortal sickness shaped themselves into clear images before his failing sight. "*There I buried Rachel,*" were among the last words on his dying lips. His eyes were dim, the forms around him were fading; his hands drooped wearily, as he left his last patriarchal blessing to his sons; but the inner eye was lighting with a strange lustre, was flashing with a glorious joy, as he saw his living Rachel, sunlit, beyond the shadows, and his arms strained forth with no faltering motion to clasp her transfigured form, and gather it to his heart of hearts.

IV. And what assures it? Whereby may I know that the vision is true? I see it. I see "the whole family" gathering there in the sunlight; strong, joyful, radiant, as men that have won a glorious victory. My heart bounds at the thought that one day I may join their company, and bear my part, a victor too, in their triumphal hymn. And whereby may I know that it is not a dream?

There are few sensitive natures, I imagine, which do not shudder sometimes with the dread of disembodiment. "*Not for that we would be unclothed,*" says the apostle, giving utterance to a great fear, which in all ages has preyed on the human heart. And there are few tender, loving hearts which do not often tremble before the question, "What if all personal links and bonds are snapped in sunder by death?" The fear of wandering forth, an exile from the flesh, a bloodless, bodiless ghost, was the great torment of the spirit, before Christ and the resurrection had been preached in the world. And the fear of losing all knowledge of dear and familiar forms, and of being cut off from all the holiest associations of this life, in eternity, has haunted the Christian ages, and has been a paralysing terror to many a true Christian heart. But these notions, the "sleep of the soul," "the disembodied state," are just the bugbears with which a narrow and hard theology has oppressed mankind. In truth, the whole mediæval conception of the world behind the veil, is set in too sad a key. The Church then used freely the tones of gloom and terror; she ruled by fear, and sought to terrify men into the deliverance which her sacraments offered. But her influence has long been waning, she seems to be settling into her second childhood; and now the gospel, whose first words are joy and hope, resumes its ministry, and good news about God, about death, about eternity, are everywhere abroad.

The soul never sleeps. There is no disembodied human spirit. The definition of man is "an embodied spirit," and it cannot be the very manhood of man that death has commission to destroy. The body that sin has corrupted, death rends in pieces and buries out of sight. Blessed be God, its pains and frets, its stormy passion, its panting lust, lie buried in the grave for ever. But a "building of God" awaits the trembling spirit in the moment of dissolution, that it may be "*not unclothed, but clothed upon,*" and that "*mortality may be swallowed up of life.*"

The witness of this is the Lord's resurrection. The gospel of those wondrous forty days which He spent with mortals after His passion, when, as Peter declared to Cornelius, "He did eat and drink with them," and when "He showed Himself unto them alive by many infallible proofs," reveals to us the embodiment of departed spirits, and unveils to us the homelikeness of the heavenly world. If He aimed at anything by those familiar appearances, in a bodily form which they could see and touch, and on which they could count the wounds, He aimed at the assurance, not of immortality only, not of resurrection only, but of the full continuity of life. All that constitutes the interest, the work, and the hope of life, is carried through the veil, and resumed with a sacred joy under the blest conditions which here we pined for—the conditions of a sinless and eternal world.

Personality obliterated! Kindred unrecognised! Love all drawn off from the creature, and lost in God! It is treason to the Man of the resurrection to imagine it. Personality will be revealed, kinship will be discovered, love will be unbound, when the blots and the blurs of evil have been purged from the spirit. We shall see then, what we knew and loved in part on earth, revealed in its wholeness, and know for the first time what to live and to love may mean. I know not what forms the recovered ones will wear. I know not how the dead are raised up, nor with what body they will come. Enough for me that the great Forerunner, the great Leader of the host, was raised in His human wholeness; each line, each touch, of His dear humanity more perfect, than when He was with us in the weakness of His mortality. The Lord took all by which man might know Him, and for which man might love Him, through death into the eternal world. He took it visibly, that we might have assurance of the Invisible; and that we might hold fast the faith, that whatever may have perished of our dear ones, whom we have loved in the Lord and lost awhile, all that made their dearness lives on, and has grown to a divine completeness under the touch of Death.

We may perchance have had some glimpse of

the image which they are wearing, in the moment when the fret and the waste of life seemed to vanish, and there fell on their faces a solemn and holy beauty, as they settled into the silence of death. One has often seen in a dying face at such moments an ideal beauty, wherein all that might be possible to the nature seemed expressed; a sign and a prophecy of eternity. Some meet tabernacle must be ready for the spirit when death unbinds it; some organ of intercourse with its fellows and with the great universe, or the triumphant language of St. Paul which we have quoted, would be a mockery and a snare. The dead even now are wearing some form, which fits them to mingle in the great congress of the first-born, already met in fellowship on high. But nothing even·there as yet seems final. The complete form of the glorified spirit, the body of the resurrection, still waits the trumpet-call of that last great day of God; the day when the work of restitution shall be finished, the day of the full and final manifestation of His sons.

And *" there they are before the throne of God, and they serve Him day and night in His temple:"* one band, once more, met again and met for ever. Hearts long sundered, knit again in immortal fellowship; the struggles and sorrows of earth their most sacred memory; "the far off interest of tears," their most dear possession; brothers of an order of which Christ is the Living Elder, and whose consecrating priest was Death.

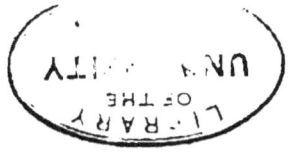

THE END.

www.ingramcontent.com/pod-product-compliance
Lightning Source LLC
Chambersburg PA
CBHW021158230426
43667CB00006B/453